The
Sales Manager's
Guide to RFPs

The Sales Manager's Guide to RFPs

How to Improve Your Win Rate
When Pursuing RFPs from
Businesses or State and Local
Government Agencies

David L. Seibert

THE SALES MANAGER'S GUIDE TO RFPs

Seibert, David. The Sales Manager's Guide to RFPs: how to improve your win rate when pursuing RFPs from businesses or state and local government agencies

ISBN-13: 979-8-9897972-0-2

Cincinnati, Ohio, United States

This book is dedicated to my five amazing grandkids:
Sawyer, Delaney, Molly, Barrett, and Boston.

Table of Contents

Executive Introduction 1

DESIGNING AND BUILDING YOUR SALES PROCESS 7

1. The RFP Selling Process — An Overview 9
   - *Overview: The RFP Selling Process™* 10
   - *Phase 1: Prospecting for new opportunities* 12
   - *Phase 2: Pre-RFP selling* 13
   - *Phase 3: Proposal planning and development* 14
   - *Phase 4: Post-proposal selling* 16
   - *Phase 5: Post-proposal research and analysis* 17
   - *Making the RFP Selling Process™ your own* 19

2. Design Considerations When Configuring Your Sales Process 21
   - *1. There are always multiple buyers* 22
   - *2. Buyers form opinions before the RFP is released* 24
   - *3. Buyers want to meet with operations staff and SME's* 26
   - *4. Buyers want transparency and accountability* 28
   - *5. Some decision makers may not understand what they're buying* ... 29
   - *6. Differentiation is critical to your success* 31
   - *7. Price is always important, but the best price doesn't always win* 32
   - *8. The selection process changes by organization* 34
   - *9. Individual motivations drive organizational requirements* 35
   - *10. You aren't always done once the proposal is submitted* 38

PHASE 1: PROSPECTING FOR NEW OPPORTUNITIES 41

3. Prospecting for Recurring Programs 43
   - *Finding recurring programs to pursue* 44
   - *Researching contracts* 48
   - *Expand your universe of opportunities* 53
   - *Prospecting for contacts* 54

4. Prospecting for One-Time Projects and Acquisitions 57
   - *Building one-to-one buyer relationships* 58

PHASE 2: PRE-RFP SELLING 63

5. Pre-RFP Selling: The Big Picture 65

Why pre-RFP selling takes so long 65

Sales strategy: the big picture 67

6. Building Your Brand and Reputation in the Market 69

7. Pre-RFP Selling Part 1: Learning About Them 75

Identify and get to know all of the decision makers 77

Document buyer requirements, objectives, and the motivations that prompted them 79

Why are they going out to bid now? 81

Document their decision model and criteria 84

How important is price? 86

8. Pre-RFP Selling Part 2: Educating Them About You 87

Getting in front of buyers—face-to-face meetings 88

Staying in front of buyers—selling tools 90

Warning: Don't talk about solutions too early 99

9. Pre-RFP Selling Part 3: Wrap-up and Recommendations 103

Discovery status meeting 104

What recommendations do you want to make? 108

Make a targeted selling plan for the next few months 109

Appreciate what you've accomplished 110

PHASE 3: PROPOSAL PLANNING AND DEVELOPMENT 111

10. Bid/No Bid Decision Making 113

1. Buyer familiarity 116

2. Requirements and capabilities 120

3. Competitive position 121

4. Production capacity 123

5. Proposal team capacity 124

6. Profitability 125

Putting it all together 125

How to No-Bid 126

11. Scrutinizing the RFP 129

Is the RFP what you expected? 129

Are there any "showstoppers"? 130

What are the major requirements and specifications? 130

How do they evaluate / score proposals? 131

Is there any language favoring a competitor? 131

What has changed from their last RFP to this one? 132

Are there any items that are not clear? 133

12. Proposal Kickoff Meeting Part 1: Compiling and
Analyzing What You've Learned 135
   Compiling and sharing what you know 136
   Processing Information into Intelligence 139
   Actionable intelligence is your objective 144
13. Proposal Kickoff Meeting Part 2: Configuring Your
Solution.. 145
   Why is all this important in an RFP/proposal context? 147
14. Proposal Kickoff Meeting Part 3: Configuring Your
Sales Message 151
   Process and outcome 151
   Questions to ask and answer 154

PHASE 4: POST-PROPOSAL SELLING 169

15. Presentation Development 171
   Ensuring sales messaging continuity 171
   Buyers want to hear from operations staff 172
   How to structure your presentation 174
   Presentation tips 177

**PHASE 5: POST-PROPOSAL RESEARCH AND
ANALYSIS 179**

16. Debrief Your Staff 181
17. Calculating Win Rates 183
   Other ways to calculate win ratios 189
18. Request copies of competitive proposals 191
   Analyzing other vendors' proposals 193
   Doing a deep dive against a competitive proposal 196
19. Conduct Post-Decision Interviews with Buyers 197

ADDITIONAL SELLING SCENARIOS 203

20. Recompetes When You Are the Incumbent 205
   Incumbent vendors have a big advantage 206
   How to win more recompetes 208
21. How to Handle RFPs You Weren't Expecting 215
   Evaluate your situation 216
   Consider your options 218
   Schedule a 'streamlined' kickoff meeting 224

REFERENCE 225

Glossary 227
Recommended Reading 239
Index 241

Executive Introduction

The problem with most books about RFPs and proposals is they're too focused on RFPs and proposals. They're too focused on the writing part, not the selling part. They discuss proposal strategy but not sales strategy. They document what you should be doing in the days after an RFP is received, but often ignore the months and years before it's published.

This book is different.

The purpose of this book is to *refocus* salespeople on selling, to *refocus* them on the months and years before the RFP is published, and to *refocus* them on all of the many selling tasks that have to happen during that time.

I emphasize that word, *refocus,* because whenever RFPs are involved, that's exactly what too many salespeople and sales managers lose—*their focus.*

Disciplined selling

When I was a rookie salesperson and took a new opportunity to my manager because I wanted to invest resources in it, they always asked the same question: "Is it qualified?" This is sales jargon. Qualifying an opportunity means evaluating it against objective criteria to determine whether it is worth investing the time and effort to pursue.

This initial question was always followed by a barrage of more specific questions:

- Is it a good fit for what we're selling?
- Are you working with someone who has authority to make buying decisions?
- Do they have budget money available to fund the purchase?

- Do they have a timeframe for purchasing and implementing the service? Or are they just kicking tires?
- Are they using our competitor's product now? If so, why are they talking to us?

The list goes on but the message is clear; as salespeople, we were not permitted to use scarce organizational resources haphazardly, without a plan or purpose. If we wanted to invest resources, we first had to build a business case that justified their use. We had to meet a standard, we were subject to oversight and, ultimately, we were held accountable for how we used those resources. As professional sellers, we were committed to a process that we knew—that precedent had proven—would produce consistently better outcomes.

We were focused.

Sellers lose their focus when they get an RFP

While most veteran sales professionals agree that qualifying sales opportunities is a best practice, all that good sense seems to dissipate the moment a new RFP lands on somebody's desk.

"Ooh, look, an RFP. Let's respond."

For too many salespeople and sales managers, deciding whether to respond to an RFP is not a decision, it's more of a reflex. And in their Pavlovian-like rush to utter those words, "Let's respond!" nobody takes the time to ask that all important question: *"Is it qualified?"*

Nobody asks, *"Is it a good fit for what we do?"*

Nobody asks, *"Are they working with one of our competitors?"*

Nobody asks, *"Do we have a relationship with anyone at this organization?"*

Nobody asks, *"Do we know any of the decision makers? Or the influencers? Do we even know who those people are?"*

Even though nobody asks any of those questions, undisciplined sellers start throwing resources at the RFP. They consume a lot of time from a lot of people, cobble together a proposal, and then they submit it. And then they lose. And then they wonder why.

The good news is we don't have to wonder why they lose because we already know. They lose because they're being reactive instead of proactive. Instead of going out ahead of time and finding opportunities and qualifying them and developing them and doing all the things that salespeople ought to do—*that salespeople are supposed to do*—they wait for an RFP to fall in their lap and then react to it. They've lost their focus.

It is precisely this loss of focus that explains why their win rates are so low, and it is precisely why they need to *refocus* on selling.

Put selling back in the sales process!

Don't misunderstand the point; proposals are integral and mandatory—*you cannot win formal procurements without them*—but they are only one discrete part of much larger buying and selling processes that begin long before the RFP is released and continue after your proposal is submitted. And that's the part salespeople need to refocus on—the selling that has to happen before the RFP is received and after the proposal is submitted.

> Salespeople have to make the sale whether or not an RFP is involved.

Too many professional salespeople have been lulled or hoodwinked into believing that an RFP replaces traditional seller and buyer interaction. It doesn't. It never has. *Salespeople still have to make the sale whether or not an RFP is involved.*

Implementing an RFP selling process

If you pursue formal procurements, stop being reactive. Stop wasting your time and your company's resources chasing RFPs you aren't expecting, aren't prepared for, and have little or no chance of winning. It's the business development equivalent of school kids chasing rabbits around a field. Sure, they may catch one every once in a while—usually when a kid trips at the same time the rabbit stumbles—but most of the rabbits are going to get away. The bad part is they get away only after you've spent a lot of time, effort, and money chasing them.

If you're serious about improving your win rate, you need to be disciplined. You need to design and build a selling process that is well aligned with the formal procurement buying processes your customers are using.

You need to be proactive, too. You need to identify opportunities ahead of time, meet with decision makers and influencers, take subject matter experts to meet with decision makers and influencers, understand the buyer's projects and programs, understand the buyer's conflicts and limitations and, in general, do all of the things that salespeople are supposed to do to win new business.

If you do all of these things—if you are disciplined, if you are proactive, if you put selling back into the selling process—your win rate will go up. If you do these things well, your win rate will go up significantly. If you don't, it won't.

It really is that simple.

WHO THIS BOOK IS FOR

Most of the sales managers and salespeople I've met in my consulting practice already know how to sell. They've read books, taken classes, studied various selling methodologies, and spent lots of time in the trenches learning the ins and outs of the selling profession. They've already developed the knowledge and skills they need to be effective salespeople. They already know how to:

- **Prospect** for new opportunities using email, phone, direct mail, and other methods.
- **Network** through an organization to identify decision makers, decision influencers, and naysayers.
- **Interview** buyers with the ideal combination of open-ended and close-ended questions to most effectively identify buyer needs and issues.

- **Listen** to buyers' answers to *really hear* what they're saying and uncover the things they don't say out loud.
- **Present** persuasively structured explanations to influence buyers to adopt a particular approach.

The point is most of these sales professionals already know how to sell. So when I encounter a sales manager or salesperson who is struggling with low RFP win rates, it doesn't take much scrutiny to discover their problem is usually not related to a lack of leadership skills or sales ability. More often, all they need is some education about the formal procurement process. They need to learn how to both navigate it and capitalize on the opportunities it presents.

That is precisely what this book is about. It is not "Selling 101," it does not try to teach you the basic selling skills you already know. This book is about helping experienced sales professionals apply their already acquired skills and knowledge to first understand and then capitalize on the formal procurement process.

A comment about terminology

Organizations with lots of experience pursuing formal procurements use sophisticated processes and terminology—such as pursuit, capture and capture planning, pre-sales, color team reviews, discriminators, compliance matrices—that are largely unique to the formal procurement world. Salespeople who are transitioning from other non-RFP markets tend to use other terminology.

I purposefully chose to use the language and terminology that transitioning salespeople are most familiar with in an effort to ease the transition and minimize the risk of confusion.

I hope you enjoy the book, and I hope you profit from it.

Designing and Building Your Sales Process

There are many things to consider when pursuing formal procurements. First and most fundamental is making sure your selling process aligns with their buying process.

1.

The RFP Selling Process—An Overview

In the world of professional selling, there's no such thing as a universal, one-size-fits-all selling process. To the contrary, the selling process you implement must match the buying process your customers are using in the same way an electric plug should match the socket you intend to plug it into. You can't put a 110V plug into a 220V outlet, and you can't use a generic selling process in response to a formal procurement.

Consider this real-world example. If you own a store that sells office supplies, would you treat local businesses the same as retail consumers? Would you make them go to your retail store to buy supplies? No! If you were smart, you'd hire a dedicated salesperson to setup commercial accounts for local businesses, and then you'd offer things like volume discounts, free local delivery, and various bonus programs that encourage your business customers to use more of your services and buy more of your office products. You'd do these things because your business customers are not retail customers; they require a unique selling process that is better suited to how they buy and encourages them to buy more.

A unique selling process for formal procurements

Now let's apply the same logic to formal procurements and RFPs. Many organizations *mandate* that formal procurements be used when buying high value or mission critical goods and services. In other words, managers in these organizations do not have a choice; they cannot buy goods and services without first organizing a procurement and issuing an RFP. And it's not just one or two buyers here or there, either. Tens of thousands of organizations are compelled by law, regulation, or company policy to use formal procurements:

- State and local government agencies.
- Schools, libraries, and other organizations funded by state or local government money.
- Businesses that work on publicly-funded projects in which they subcontract portions of their work to other businesses.
- Medium and large businesses that enforce strict procurement policies to ensure funds are used wisely and purchases are consistent with organizational goals and objectives.
- All major federal government procurements.

If you do business with any of these types of organizations, you need to recognize that formal procurements are the rule, not the exception. If you want to make lots of sales, consistently, you need to configure your selling approach to match the formal procurement processes your customers are using. You need to create your own RFP selling process.

OVERVIEW: THE RFP SELLING PROCESS™

It's always easier to create a new business process if you've got something to start with. That's why I created *The RFP Selling Process™*. The process should not be implemented as it's presented on these pages; you have to create your own. But it is a prototype you can use as a guide to design and build your own selling process that is correctly sized and configured for your business and the resources you have available.

The RFP Selling Process™ is organized into five phases, each of which is preceded by an event that triggers it. It also includes a variety of tasks that should be completed in each phase.

Event: Decision to be proactive		
Phase 1: **Prospecting for New Opportunities**	Ongoing	• Identify recurring programs that will be rebid. • Search for organizations that will launch projects. • Create new projects or programs.
Event: Opportunity identified		
Phase 2: **Pre-RFP Selling**	12 – 24 Months	• Identify and network with decision makers and influencers. • Document the opportunity. • Pursue discovery, investigation, and education. • Build strong relationships. • Establish the credibility of your team. • Create solutions to buyer problems. • Gain organization-wide support for solutions. • Identify antagonists.
Event: RFP released		
Phase 3: **Proposal Development**	½ – 2 months	• Configure solution. • Configure messaging. • Configure pricing. • Develop, produce, and deliver proposal.
Event: Proposal submitted		
Phase 4: **Post-Proposal Selling**	1–3 months	• Post proposal presentation. • Final negotiation.
Event: Decision made		
Phase 5: **Post-Proposal Research & Analysis Phase**	1-6 months	• Recalculate win ratios. • Debrief buyer representatives (win or loss). • Interview business development staff. • Acquire copies of competitive proposals. • Perform competitive assessment.

PHASE 1: PROSPECTING FOR NEW OPPORTUNITIES

If you want to improve your win rate when pursuing new business, you have to be proactive. This necessarily means you have to commit to regular and routine prospecting. You have to find opportunities so you can start working them while there is still time to convince the buyer that you are the best vendor and you have the best solution for their needs.

Whenever I talk about being proactive, about finding opportunities ahead of time, someone almost always objects: "How can we possibly know about an RFP before it's released?" Here's the answer.

Salespeople need to stop focusing so much on the RFP and start focusing on the opportunity it represents. Focusing on the RFP is like focusing on the last 100 yards of a marathon without considering the 26 miles that came before. It's backwards.

Begin at the beginning

Salespeople need to refocus their efforts on the beginning of the race. They need to refocus on finding opportunities and working them at those early stages where they actually have an opportunity to influence the outcome.

Lewis Carroll: "Begin at the beginning."

As professional salespeople, a big part of your job is going out, meeting and interacting with the people in the markets you're selling into, and then finding existing opportunities or creating new opportunities you can develop into sales.

An RFP doesn't change any of that.

Whether or not an RFP is involved, you still have to go out and network for potential buyers and prospect for potential opportunities. That's your job. It's what you do. It's why you're paid so well.

I get it, prospecting is arduous work, and it requires the ongoing commitment of dedicated salespeople. But if your sales organization makes the commitment to prospecting, and your salespeople are steadfast at implementing the plan, you and your team can begin working opportunities long before your competitors know about them, and long before the RFP comes out. And that, more than anything else you do, will improve your win rate.

PHASE 2: PRE-RFP SELLING

Once an opportunity is identified, salespeople launch their selling effort, often referred to as *discovery*. I call it 'Mutual Discovery' because that's what it is. Mutual Discovery is a two-way street—it's you learning about them just as much as them learning about you—and it involves many things.

- Identifying and then networking with decision makers and influencers.
- Documenting all aspects of the project or program.
- Educating buyers about your product or service, and sharing other relevant industry information that will make you a valuable information resource.
- Building strong relationships with everyone in their organization who is or may be involved in the procurement decision.
- Encouraging interaction between your subject matter experts and theirs, and working to establish the credibility of your entire team.
- Creating solutions to buyer problems.
- Gaining organization wide support for the solutions you recommend.
- Identifying antagonists who would derail your efforts.

I could go on, but you get the idea. This is the phase where salespeople figure out who's who and what's what, and the buyer figures out who you are, what you offer, and whether they can trust you to deliver on the promises you make.

Seeking multiple, interconnected relationships

One of the *biggest differences* between formal procurement processes and other less formal buying processes is the depth of interaction that needs to happen between the two organizations. Whenever it involves projects or programs that are expensive, high profile, or mission critical — and most formal procurements are — *buyers want to talk with SMEs and operations staff.* They want to talk with the people they're going to be working with who are going to be delivering the product or service they're buying.

- **It's good** if your salesperson engages with a decision maker.
- **It's better** if your salesperson engages with multiple decision makers and influencers.
- **It's best** if your salesperson takes your SMEs and your operations staff to engage with the buyer's decision makers, SMEs, and operations staff. The more interconnected relationships there are, the more everybody gets to know and trust everybody else, the better your chances of winning their business.

If you've identified this opportunity early on, the mutual discovery phase can easily span 12-24 months before the RFP is released.

PHASE 3: PROPOSAL PLANNING AND DEVELOPMENT

Once an RFP is released, the project moves into the proposal development phase.

I've made clear this book is about the selling part of the formal procurement process, not the writing part. This is still true. But it's important to understand that salespeople play an important role in the proposal development phase.

An RFP is not a questionnaire

Far too often, I've seen salespeople toss an RFP over a cubicle wall to a proposal writer, and as they're disappearing around the corner, they yell over their shoulder, "*Make us look good.*"

OK, I exaggerate.

But not by much.

In far too many cases, salespeople handoff an RFP to the proposal team, but don't give them any background on the buyer, who they are, what they want, what they care about, or provide any other relevant information that would allow the proposal writers to customize the response to the buyer's actual needs. They do this because they're treating the RFP like it's a simple questionnaire, an administrative item that needs to get checked off someone's to-do list.

They're wrong.

An RFP is _not_ a questionnaire disconnected from the larger buying and selling process, and the proposal you write in response, therefore, cannot be just a bunch of stock answers. A proposal should be a restatement of what's been discussed, a culmination of everything you've been talking about with the buyer during the course of the pre-RFP selling effort. It's where you put in writing everything that's been discussed verbally.

Think '_message continuity._'

To be successful, you absolutely must maintain a consistent message from the pre-RFP selling phase to the proposal phase to the post-proposal presentation phase—if it goes that far. This is why it is critical that salespeople be intrinsically involved in proposal development.

Salespeople play an important role in proposal development

Proposal writers cannot write compelling, buyer-focused content if they don't know what the buyer wants. Therefore, salespeople must invest lots of time and effort making sure everyone on the team—including the proposal manager, proposal writers, and subject matter experts—have been thoroughly briefed on the opportunity.

1. **Share information about the buyer and what they want.** The salesperson needs to brief the proposal team about individual decision makers and influencers and what they each care about, the scope of the project, the buyer's relationship with other vendors, etc.

2. **Document the solution**. The team, led by the salesperson, and in cooperation with subject matter experts, has to configure and document the actual solution they are proposing.

3. **Agree on messaging**. The team, led by the salesperson, and in cooperation with subject matter experts, has to hammer out the messaging they want to use to most effectively communicate about the solution.

4. **Configure pricing.** Someone, either in cooperation with or led by the salesperson, has to figure out how much you're going to charge for the solution you're providing.

In my experience, most proposal writers can work some incredible magic with your sales message, but they can't do it if they've never been fully briefed on the opportunity. By leading these briefings, your salespeople are doing their part to ensure the proposal you submit is relevant and compelling to the reviewers who will evaluate it.

PHASE 4: POST-PROPOSAL SELLING

The actual selection process buyers use will often change based on the goods being procured, the strategic importance of the goods being procured, and the organization's policies. There are a variety of different scenarios.

- An organization will evaluate each proposal and choose one vendor; the best proposal wins.
- The buyer selects your firm, but now you have to discuss, negotiate, and hammer out the final contract terms.
- The selection team will evaluate the proposals, and then the top three or four vendors will be invited onsite to deliver a presentation to the buyer's team. The best presenter wins.
- The buyer chooses the vendor they want, and then launches a 'due diligence' investigation on certain critical items. If the vendor is going to be hosting consumer data on their systems, for example, the buyer will complete a thorough assessment to ensure all of the necessary security systems are in place and functioning.
- Some combination of the above.

The point is you aren't necessarily done when the proposal is submitted. There are typically other steps that have to happen before the contract gets signed.

The important thing for salespeople to remember is that the team helped get you to this point, so now is not the time to jettison their involvement and 'go it alone.' I say this because a lot of salespeople have a habit of saying, "OK, thanks for the proposal, I got it from here." And then they go off and deliver a presentation that is too often disconnected from the messaging you configured in the previous steps.

Again, think *"message continuity."*

Instead of your salesperson going it alone at this critical stage, it's vital to include the rest of the team both in the creation of the presentation and choosing who will be onsite delivering the presentation. As much as most salespeople like to present, most buyers want to hear from the operations staff who will be managing their projects. This is an important idea, one you need to embrace and not dismiss.

> As much as most salespeople like to present, most buyers want to hear from the operations staff who will be managing their projects.

If you take great care at this critical step, if you involve more of your team in the post proposal effort, you will improve your win rate.

PHASE 5: POST-PROPOSAL RESEARCH AND ANALYSIS

One of the things that differentiates true professionals from perpetual rookies is their commitment to learning from past performance. Perpetual rookies don't spend much time reviewing their performance or analyzing their successes and losses. As a result, they keep making the same mistakes and missing out on the same opportunities—over and over and over again.

Professionals, in contrast, take time to review their past performance and analyze their successes and losses. They learn from their losses as well as their successes.

This continual self-evaluation allows professionals to improve because it informs them where they're doing well, where they're falling short, and what they need to do to get better and win more. As you build your selling process, it's important to include post-proposal research and analysis. This usually includes four important parts.

1. Conduct a post-proposal debrief with your internal team

Your business development team (which includes salespeople, proposal managers, proposal writers, subject matter experts, and a few others) already have great insights into what's working internally and what's not working so well. Don't forget to ask them what they think.

2. Conduct post-proposal debrief with the buyer

Many buyers are more than willing to share feedback with sellers about the proposals they submitted, all you have to do is ask. If you choose the right person to conduct the interviews, and if you really, truly open your mind to the feedback the buyer provides, you're going to learn some valuable things that will help you in future procurements.

3. Collect and analyze competitive proposals

U.S. states have laws or regulations, similar to the federal government's Freedom of Information Act (FOIA), that require agencies to disclose records to people who request them. Fortunately for sellers, this includes proposals that vendors submit in response to RFPs. Requesting copies of these proposals allows you to learn more about your competitors, how they're positioning their products, and how they're positioning themselves against their competitors.

Having access to competitive proposals is one of the most valuable assets you can accumulate when competing against other vendors.

4. Calculate win ratios

Most sellers can *more or less* give you a *basic* win rate statistic. When I say "more or less," I mean they *may* have calculated their win rate, but often as not, they *may* be guessing. When I say "basic," I mean they're only calculating one win rate; how many opportunities they've won vs. how many RFPs they bid on. I refer to this win rate as the Gross Proposal Win Rate.

The Gross Proposal Win Rate can give you some basic insights into how well you're doing, especially when you're tracking it over time, but not a lot more. The good news is there are a whole bunch of other win rates you can track—all without too much effort—that can give you much more insight into which parts of your selling effort are doing well and which need work.

Taking the time to calculate your win rates is a vital tool for sales managers who want to get better.

MAKING THE RFP SELLING PROCESS™ YOUR OWN

I explained in the beginning of this chapter that the RFP Selling Process™ is a model, a prototype that you have to customize so it reflects the unique characteristics of your industry and works well within your organization.

The chapter you're just completing is an overview intended to show you the forest for the trees, the 30,000-foot view. The rest of this book describes the RFP Selling Process™ in more detail. Its purpose is to give you the insights you need to ask the right questions and consider the various decisions you'll have to make as you design and build your own RFP selling process and infrastructure.

2.

Design Considerations When Configuring Your Sales Process

In the previous chapter, we discussed The RFP Selling Process™ and how you should use it as a prototype, a starting point, from which you build your own RFP selling program that works for your business and your industry.

As you work to design and build your program, it's important to first recognize and then account for the character, nature, and nuances associated with the formal procurement process. Only by understanding these things can you align your selling processes so they work well with your customers' buying processes.

Ten characteristics of formal procurements

Listed here are the ten most important characteristics of formal procurements that you must account for as you design and implement your selling process:

1. There are always multiple buyers.
2. Buyers form opinions before the RFP is released.
3. Buyers want to meet with operations staff and subject matter experts.
4. Buyers want transparency and accountability.

---

5. Some decision makers may not understand what you're selling (or what they're buying).
6. Differentiation is critical to your success.
7. Price is always important, but the best price doesn't always win.
8. The selection process varies by organization.
9. Individual motivations drive organizational requirements.
10. You aren't always done once the proposal is submitted.

In the rest of this chapter, we explore each characteristic in more detail. We also explore what sellers need to do to align with each.

1. THERE ARE ALWAYS MULTIPLE BUYERS

Since the beginning of time, sales professionals have been schooled to always search out the decision maker, the person who has buying authority. It's good advice, too. Far too many sales rookies have wasted far too much time talking with friendly "buyers" who express interest in a product or service, but lack the authority to buy it. It's the salesperson's version of an exercise in futility.

The same rule—*find the decision maker*—applies to formal procurements, but with a caveat. Instead of finding the decision maker, the rule is:

Find the decision makers. Plural.

In most formal procurements, there is rarely one decision maker. In most cases there are multiple people and groups involved in the decision process, and just as many who influence the decision makers. You need to find them all.

If a university is preparing to select a construction company and design firm to build a new student center, many sellers might assume the decision will be made by the President of the university or the Board of Directors. They might also seek out the Facilities Manager or Building and Grounds

Manager, the person who likely has the most experience with building construction and maintenance.

This small group might be the people who make the ultimate buying decision, who sign on the dotted line, so you definitely need to know them. But understand they are NOT the only people involved in the decision process. In fact, the procurement process the university implements will likely involve many more people and groups. These may include...

- Staff from the campus safety department who will be concerned about securing the facility and traffic flow in and around the site.
- The head of IT networking, who will have to figure out how to wire the new building for Wi-Fi.
- A representative from the compliance department because, as a result of some grants they receive, they have to ensure the new facility is energy efficient.
- A manager from the Athletic Director's office who is always interested in new amenities that will help them recruit new athletes.
- Elected representatives from local governments who want to promote new projects happening in their communities.
- Members of student council leadership who are interested in making the facility accessible and student-friendly.
- The occasional lunch lady.

As a salesperson, it's not enough to identify the senior people who make the final decision. You must identify all of the other decision makers and influencers who play a role in the decision process.

These kinds of major acquisitions never, ever happen in a vacuum. They involve a lot of people with a lot of interests. You need to know who they are—all of them—and what they care about.

Takeaway #1	*It's not enough to find "the" decision maker, you need to find the decision makers, plural. You need to identify and get to know all of the people—decision makers and influencers—involved in the decision process.*

2. BUYERS FORM OPINIONS BEFORE THE RFP IS RELEASED

When decision makers are tasked with purchasing a product or service that is strategically important or high profile, they generally perceive personal risk. After all, if you select an employee benefits vendor who ultimately doesn't do a very good job, it's going to be difficult facing your coworkers every morning when you go into work.

Acknowledging the stakes at hand, most people involved in selecting a product or service will prepare themselves for the decision they face, though their preparation will vary by person and role.

A program manager might be very involved, meet with all of the potential vendors beforehand and interview their subject matter experts. In contrast, a staffer who gets "conscripted" onto the selection committee might casually talk with their coworkers to see what considerations they think are most important. Another staffer may spend time searching the Internet to gain some insight about the product or service they're buying, the major companies in the field, etc.

However they do it, most buyers on the selection committee will approach the purchase decision with some predispositions. That's not to say they've made their final decision before the RFP is published, though some may have. But it does suggest they've probably been developing preconceptions, biases, and preferences.

So what does this mean to sellers? It means sellers have to start selling long before the RFP is published. Consider these facts.

Fact #1: you "make the sale" in the 24 months before the RFP is released

Opportunities are often won or lost in the 12-24 months before an RFP is released. This does not suggest you are actively "pitching" your product or service that entire time. You aren't.

It's during this 24-month period that sellers and buyers get to know each other. It's where salespeople should be identifying decision makers and influencers, meeting people and building relationships, and uncovering buyer problems and issues. Eventually, this is also when you are educating buyers about your organizational capabilities and staff expertise, establishing the credibility of your staff and experts, uncovering persistent buyer problems that need solutions, and in general, doing all of the things that salespeople ought to do.

It is this pre-RFP selling period where you _make_ the sale.

Fact #2: you "close the deal" in your proposal

If you are successful at making the sale before the RFP comes out, the proposal is where you "close the deal." It's where you document everything your staff and the buyer's staff have been working on and talking about over the previous 24 months. It's where you formalize your discussions into a clear, concise, and well-articulated solution with all of the i's dotted and the t's crossed.

Fact #3: you cannot "close the deal" if you don't first make the sale

You cannot close the deal until you first make the sale. This seems obvious, right? Unfortunately, this is the most common mistake that many sellers make.

Far too many sellers get an RFP _out of the blue_—one they aren't expecting or aren't prepared for—and then they say, "Hey look, an RFP. Let's respond!" Then they lose.

They lose because they're operating under the profoundly misguided belief that the proposal they write somehow replaces the larger selling process. They actually believe that a proposal, a bunch of words on paper, can somehow replace all of the discussions and discovery, all of the relationship-building and credibility-building, all of the problem-solving and solution-developing—_all of the stuff that salespeople usually invest months or years doing_. You can't replace all of those things with a proposal, no matter how well written it is.

You cannot "close the deal" unless you first "make the sale." Remember that.

Takeaway #2	*Buyers form opinions before the RFP is released. To be effective, the RFP selling process you design must begin engaging buyers in the 12-24 months before the RFP is released, during that timeframe when those buyers are forming their opinions.*

3. BUYERS WANT TO MEET WITH OPERATIONS STAFF AND SME'S

Selling within an *informal* procurement environment is much like golf—it's a solo sport. It's typically one salesperson, on their own, personally and singularly responsible for their own results. If you drive the ball 300 yards down the middle of the fairway, it's all you. If you shank the ball and dent a golf cart one fairway over, it's all you. You may engage some subject matter experts to help you from time to time but still, informal, business-to-business selling is largely a salesperson-driven, salesperson-centric, solo sport.

In contrast to informal procurements, the selling process you use when pursuing *formal* procurements is fundamentally and substantively different. And the biggest difference of all? It's a team sport. Sure, there may be one central salesperson—the quarterback who is managing the team and calling the plays—but winning in this arena necessarily requires that the entire team participate. It's an open, transparent process where lots of people are actively engaged, and the more people you involve, the better off you are. In this scenario, everyone has responsibilities and assignments, everyone is responsible for accomplishing certain tasks, and everyone contributes to the outcome.

The big reason formal procurement selling is a team sport, not a solo effort, is because the operations people in the buyer's organization don't want to work with salespeople, at least not exclusively. They want to acquaint themselves with the experts and professionals and operations staff who will actually be delivering the services they're buying.

- An IT buyer wants to talk with the seller's staff who are experts in data security.
- A compliance person in the buyer's organization wants to talk with an officer in the seller's organization who is educated on all of the applicable laws and regulations—someone who can discuss compliance.
- An administrator in the buyer's organization wants to talk with staff in the seller's organization responsible for preparing reports, generating invoices, and doing all the other things that administrators require in order to process their daily work.
- A representative of the user community wants to talk with the manager of the support department to learn how user problems are handled when they are reported.

At the end of the day, experts want to talk with other experts and specialists want to talk with other specialists.

The role of salespeople in formal procurements

Being a "salesperson" in this kind of environment is much more like project management than what most business-to-business salespeople typically associate with selling. Sure, it's still about networking through the buyer's organization and meeting all the various decision makers and influencers. But just as much, it's about ensuring all of the people in your organization also meet with all the various decision makers and influencers in the buyer's organization.

In that sense, selling in a formal procurement process is no different than being a conductor of a symphony. The conductor must find a way to bring a lot of moving parts, a lot of individual people and their instruments, into a coordinated, melodic whole. Likewise, a salesperson in this environment must find a way to bring a multi-person, interactive, interdependent cacophony of people and interests into a structured, coordinated program that earns the customer's confidence and solves the customer's problem.

As a result, a business development person who is responsible for selling in the world of formal procurements must have a very broad skill set. Over and above the basic selling skills that all salespeople must have, this person must also be part project manager. They should be someone who has the ability to coordinate a large, multi-year selling effort, among many people, from different departments, with sometime competing priorities—and do it all in an ordered and coordinated way that produces the desired result.

Takeaway #3	*To be effective, the sales process you design and the salesperson you assign must facilitate your subject matter experts meeting and interacting with the buyer's decision makers and influencers. The more interactions that occur, the more interpersonal relationships they form, the better it bodes for your chances of winning their business.*

4. BUYERS WANT TRANSPARENCY AND ACCOUNTABILITY

Due diligence is a thing. When an organization is buying a product or service that is strategically important to their mission, or really expensive, the people in charge of the purchase decision want to make certain they've done their due diligence. It's not enough to accept the assertions and promises of a well-meaning salesperson; they want to confirm for themselves that what they're buying will give them the outcomes they want. Further, they want to be able to defend their decision if something goes wrong and they, personally, are put on the hot seat.

To that end, buyers of expensive and strategically important goods and services demand complete transparency and total accountability as they're working their way through their selection process. If you claim during the sales process that your information systems are well protected against hackers and hacking attempts, you're likely going to have to prove it to a skeptical IT buyer. Ultimately, you will have to convince the buyer by sharing the different kinds of systems you've implemented. Later, perhaps during the actual RFP process, you'll likely have to document what you've previously discussed so there will be something in writing that holds you accountable for the claims you've made.

	Buyers are not willing to accept promises and claims about
	what you say you can do or are going to do, they want proof.
Takeaway	*To be effective, the sales process you design must embrace*
#4	*transparency. Supported by proof, this combination gives*
	buyers the confidence they need to trust the claims your
	team makes.

5. SOME DECISION MAKERS MAY NOT UNDERSTAND WHAT THEY'RE BUYING.

One of the big differences between informal and formal buying processes is the number and makeup of the people involved in the selection process.

Informal procurements often involve one decision maker. But as we already discussed in Takeaway #1, formal procurements often involve lots of diverse people from across the organization, some who are experts on what is being acquired and some who are not. This is important to understand because these non-experts are often tasked, alongside the experts, with evaluating vendor proposals.

This is so important for sellers to understand, to embrace, because the non-expert members on these review committees usually have an interest in what you're selling, but many lack an in-depth understanding about the intricacies of the products or services they're buying. As sellers, you need to understand that this unique arrangement is not an exception, it is normal and routine. Consider these examples.

Health benefits. If you are a municipality preparing to choose a health benefits provider, there is likely a benefits manager leading the selection process. But because the benefit plan directly impacts so many people throughout the organization, the selection committee may also include representatives of different groups or unions such as police officers, fire fighters, waste management, administrative staff, and more. The committee may also include a city manager or other elected official. The point is many of these people are not aware of the many issues involving benefits administration, including the things that you and the benefits manager know are important.

School software. If you are a school district procuring a new administrative software application, your selection committee may include administrators, teachers, parents, IT professionals, and yes, even the occasional lunch lady.

Limited scope projects. Even if the product or service is more limited in scope, like a new security platform to secure your company's data assets, the selection committee may still involve people beyond the IT department. This may include the VP of operations, the officer responsible for compliance with federal and state laws (because they're handling people's personal health or financial information), and maybe even someone from the office staff who has to train others on security processes.

The point is many people are often invited—and sometimes even conscripted—to participate on selection committees, but many are not always operationally central to, or fully informed about, the product or service being procured. As a result, the people who are reviewing your proposal may not understand all of the details, specifics, or intricacies of what you're selling.

This necessarily means that your pre-RFP sales efforts should involve reaching out to the various groups that might be involved in the selection process, learning their issues and concerns, and educating them about the important things they should consider during the selection process.

Takeaway #5	*You cannot assume the people on the selection committee know as much as you do. They probably don't. To be effective, the selling process you design must engage all of the groups who will or may be involved in the process. Further, you have to engage them at their level and "make the sale" with them before the RFP comes out.*

6. DIFFERENTIATION IS CRITICAL TO YOUR SUCCESS

The RFP process is inherently competitive, *and it's designed this way on purpose.* Competition is a powerful motivator. Whether it's professional baseball, Olympic curling, or a gymnasium full of Boy Scouts racing pinewood derby cars, competition encourages all of us to best the competition, to prevail, to win.

Major organizations figured this out. More than that, they figured out how to use it to their advantage. Get all of the relevant players in the same virtual room, goad one of them into saying, "I can do this for $100," and then sit back and watch quietly as the pressure of the situation spurs the others into a competitive frenzy:

"I can do the same thing for $90."

"I can do that plus a little extra, and I can do it all for $95."

"We can also do it for $100, but our automation means we can do twice the volume in half the time."

You get the idea. Major buyers figured out that vendors will engage in a competitive battle to win the business, and they recognized this competition would benefit them. Indeed, some of the greatest innovations in the world have come from these competitive contests.

In this kind of highly competitive environment, differentiation is key to success. Further, it spans the entire process, from the pre-RFP selling phase to the proposal development phase to post proposal follow-up.

Takeaway #6	*In highly competitive environments — like formal procurements — you are either effective at differentiating your solution from others or you are dismissed as a commodity. To be effective, the selling process you design must have obsessive focus on differentiating your solution.*

7. PRICE IS ALWAYS IMPORTANT, BUT THE BEST PRICE DOESN'T ALWAYS WIN

When I teach classes on how to respond to RFPs, there is always at least one person who is adamant that price is the only factor in determining whether you win or lose. According to this view, a proposal is nothing more than a vehicle to deliver pricing; a fancy wrapper that has no intrinsic value aside from the pricing information it contains.

I couldn't disagree more.

Putting price in perspective

When I encounter someone who thinks price is the only buying criteria, I challenge them to justify the existence of Cadillac®, Mercedes Benz®, Lexus®, and all other luxury automobile brands. There are many fine, dependable, feature-filled automobiles that are available for far less money than what you would spend on a high-end luxury vehicle. So why spend over $70,000 on a luxury car when you can get a perfectly reliable alternative for half the price?

And what about wrist watches? Timex® has developed a reputation based on reliability and dependability. Many of their watches are also very stylish and handsome, and they are available at reasonable prices. If price is the only buying criteria, justify the existence of Rolex®, Breitling®, Cartier®, and others. If price is the only buying criteria, why aren't we all walking around with a Timex?

Consider brand name products versus generics. When you go to the grocery store, you can buy a name brand product or you can buy a generic store brand—typically just as good, often made by the same manufacturers as the name brands, and usually for a lot less money. If price is the only consideration, then everyone would be buying off-brands, and name brand products would be a thing of the past—a quaint memory like the milkman and candy cigarettes. So why do people regularly pay more money for name brand products?

The answer to all these questions is simple; price isn't the only thing people consider when buying things.

Price is important, but it's not the only thing

Don't misunderstand the point; I am not minimizing the importance of price. *Price is important.* Price will always be important. Indeed, the single most fundamental premise underlying all economic theory is that people will do what is in their own best interest, and by extension, people generally won't pay a higher price for something if they think they can get the same thing for less somewhere else. It's just that price isn't the only criterion people use when making a purchase decision. There are times people will pay more, sometimes substantially more, if they believe they're getting more.

The trick is to know the buyer's thinking

The trick is knowing when price is the biggest issue, or the only issue, and when it's just one of many issues the buyer is considering. That knowledge only comes from knowing the buyer, of course—and knowing them really, really well. Regardless of how difficult it is to get this information, though, it's fundamental because it plays into your overall sales strategy.

If price is the primary issue, and you want to win the contract, don't waste time on lots of other stuff. Write enough to satisfy their minimum requirements, and then sharpen your pencil to provide them with the lowest possible price. Or walk away.

If price is just one of many issues, then do your best to prioritize and put your best solution forward.

Takeaway #7	*Buyers usually have many objectives when they issue RFPs, and price is usually only one of them. To be effective, your selling process should identify what's most important to the buyer so you can configure your solution to give them what they want, whether that's a low price or something else.*

8. THE SELECTION PROCESS CHANGES BY ORGANIZATION

In the world of formal procurements, RFPs in particular, there is no single method buyers use to select a vendor.

Among commercial buyers, the selection process is usually different from one company to the next, and sometimes even from one procurement to the next. Procurement processes are usually determined by internal company policies, or dictated by external regulations if they sell their product to a government entity.

Among state and local government buyers, the selection process is unique to each state, and is usually codified by law or regulation. Procurement officers usually have little flexibility to alter the terms of the acquisition; they are obligated to follow the rules that were set.

There is no universal list of selection methods, but the following is a good representation of some more common methods you'll find among state and local government and commercial buyers.

- Lowest price technically acceptable (LPTA). Of the proposals that meet minimum requirements, the one with the lowest price wins.
- A committee assigns points to each section, the points are added up, and the proposal with the most points wins.
- A committee makes recommendations to a decision maker who then makes the final decision.
- Proposal sections are assigned to internal experts who then evaluate and make recommendations only about that section.

These are just a few, but you get the idea; the way an organization buys a product or service can vary significantly.

Match your selling process to their buying process

The challenge for salespeople is to identify the type of selection process the buyer is using. You do this so you're able to organize your efforts to capitalize on, get the most benefit from, the selection process they've chosen.

For example, if a buyer is using the lowest price technically acceptable approach for a particular procurement, don't waste your time demonstrating your differentiators and business strengths, the superiority of your methods or the expertise of your staff. None of that matters. So long as you meet their minimum requirements, the only thing that matters is your price.

If a buyer is using a committee approach, in contrast, where multiple people are involved in grading your proposal and awarding points, your job is very different. In this scenario, it's important to get out and meet all of the decision makers and influencers, and take your SMEs to meet the decision makers and influencers. This is where you have to invest time selling and making the sale before the RFP comes out. And in your proposal, you have to emphasize the strengths you offer and how your solution is different and better than what anyone else is offering.

Match your selling process to their selection process.

Takeaway #8	*Buyers use various methods to select which solution and vendor they want. It's critical that sellers understand what those selection methods are because they allow you to choose the most effective selling strategy.*

9. INDIVIDUAL MOTIVATIONS DRIVE ORGANIZATIONAL REQUIREMENTS

The requirements listed in an RFP don't just happen, they all grow out of some issue or concern—a personal motivation—that someone on the buyer's staff thinks is sufficiently important that it should be included in the project's requirements. This motivation is then transformed and "sanitized" into an RFP requirement. The problem is the requirement, as articulated in the RFP, doesn't always faithfully represent the true character of the motivation that prompted it.

The following table describes personal motivations I've encountered over the years, and how those motivations were ultimately expressed in an RFP.

The buyer's personal motivation	How the motivation was expressed in the RFP
My wife and I have hit a rough spot. I need to spend more time at home, and less time managing a great big, never-ending implementation.	The winning bidder will propose a solution that must be fully implemented within three business days during normal business hours.
I'm three years away from retirement and a sweet pension. There's no way I'm going out on a limb for something unproven, no matter what the potential upside is.	Extra points will be awarded to the bidder who presents a proven, mature application that is shown, through multiple implementations, to be reliable and dependable.
The last time I picked a vendor without buy-in from my user community, I heard about it for the next three months. They have to approve it, too.	User satisfaction is critical. The winning bidder must propose a program that is easy to use by all stakeholders within our user community.

It's important to recognize that, while organizational objectives can be so general they could almost be cut and pasted across many different RFPs from as many buyers, every motivation is unique to a person. Understand the motive and you will have a much better understanding about the RFP verbiage it morphs into.

Some motivations don't become organizational objectives

While many personal motivations are transformed into organizational objectives that eventually appear in RFPs, some never make it that far. For example, I was working once with a young manager who had great aspirations and was eager to move up in his organization. More than anything, he wanted recognition. More than anything, I wanted to make a sale.

One of my more experienced associates came up with the brilliant idea to write a case study showcasing this young manager and his plans to use our product to transform productivity within his department. We even put his picture on the front of the document, making it look like an article you might find in a trade magazine. This gave us another case study we could use, but more important, it gave him the exposure he wanted. We sent him a stack of the glossy documents, and he enthusiastically shared them around the office. He got the recognition he wanted and we made a sale.

The point of this story is motivations are personal and don't always translate into an RFP objective, but they are no less important. If you understand a person's personal motivation, and you can somehow address it, you are able to give them what they really want even though no other vendor responding to the RFP knows it's an issue.

How do you learn what each decision maker's motivations are?

How do you discover their motivations? This question is, at the same time, one of the easiest questions to answer and one of the most difficult selling tasks you face.

If you want to learn what the decision maker's motivations are, you need to build a relationship with the decision maker. You need to get to know them personally. This doesn't happen overnight. Indeed, it doesn't happen unless you've developed a relationship with them and, over time, they come to trust you.

In the first example in the preceding table, the man shared something with me that was deeply personal—that he and his wife were having difficulties in their relationship. He never would have shared that if he hadn't known me, if we weren't already friends, and if he hadn't trusted me.

The point is you can't just swoop in and expect someone to share their personal thoughts and feelings and motivations with you. Building a relationship takes time.

If you want to write customer-focused proposals, if you want to understand the buyer's true motivations, you have to start calling on accounts in the 24 months before the RFP comes out. Only then will you have the time needed to gain someone's confidence and truly understand what they truly care about. You have to invest the time.

Takeaway #9	*The information you read in an RFP is sanitized corporate-speak. Reading it lets you understand the requirement, but not why it's a requirement or what prompted it. If you understand why the requirement is there, your solutions will be more targeted to their real needs and your proposal content will be more focused on them.*

10. YOU AREN'T ALWAYS DONE ONCE THE PROPOSAL IS SUBMITTED

Some buyers use a multi-step procurement process that requires an onsite presentation by sellers. The way it typically works is the buyer reviews all of the proposals they receive, ranks them, and then invites the top two or three vendors for an onsite vendor presentation. This is often referred to as "advancing to the short list."

In far too many cases, sellers respond by sending the lead salesperson. The problem with this approach is buyers don't necessarily want to talk to the salesperson, they want to evaluate the people they're going to be working with. If they haven't already, they want to get to know the operations staff who will actually be providing the services.

If you advance to the short list, it's important you include the operations staff and subject matter experts who will be working on or directly overseeing the program.

Why do buyers take this extra step? They invite you onsite because they want to know if you're legit. They want to evaluate the veracity of all the claims you make in your proposal. And the way they do it is by talking with your staff, by asking them questions and listening to their answers, and by watching their body language and considering their demeanor while they answer.

What they *really* want to know is whether you're the real deal or if you just look good on paper. And the only way they can do that is by talking—face to face—with the people on your team.

Takeaway #10	*If the buyer includes a post-proposal, onsite presentation in their buying process, then everything you've done up to this point—including your pre-RFP selling work and the proposal you submitted—is prologue. It's the necessary preparatory steps to get you to this important client meeting.*
	Don't stop selling, yet.
	You could have the greatest product, the most incredible solution, the best, most competitive price, but none of that matters if you can't close the deal here. This is your opportunity to highlight your staff's credibility and convince the buyer you can deliver everything you've promised.
	Do it well.

Phase 1:
Prospecting for New
Opportunities

In the world of formal procurements, prospecting for opportunities can mean very different things based on the type of product or service being procured. In general, there are two types of procurements sellers see most frequently, recurring programs and one-time projects.

- **Prospecting for recurring programs.** This usually involves things like employee benefit programs, payroll programs, or program management services. They are "recurring" because they are usually contracted for a few years and then go back out to market to be rebid.

- **Prospecting for one-time projects.** This usually involves projects like construction services or program development services. Once the project is completed or the acquisition is made, the contract is done.

The next two chapters discuss ways to prospect for recurring programs and one-time projects, and they explore how you prospect for each type.

3.

Prospecting for Recurring Programs

A recurring program involves a program that is periodically rebid. The way it typically works is an RFP is issued, vendors respond with a proposal, and one vendor is then chosen to provide the services. After a set period of time—usually three to five years for most state or local government contracts—the program goes back out to be rebid and the process starts over.

If you are a salesperson pursuing contracts for recurring programs, your job is both easy and hard.

It's easy because, since these kinds of programs go back out to be rebid on a fairly regular basis, there is a steady stream of opportunities for you to find and pursue. With dedicated staff and diligent effort, you should be able to identify most or all of the contracts in your field.

It's hard because, since the contracts are generally well known in the market, your competitors will also be pursuing them. This means there's lots of competition and noise you have to cut through if you're going to convince the buyers your solution is best for them.

Let's explore.

FINDING RECURRING PROGRAMS TO PURSUE

There are six fundamental ways to identify potential recurring programs before an RFP is published:

1. Keep and log every RFP you receive.
2. Build target profiles to identify organizations similar to your existing customers who may require similar services.
3. Talk with industry consultants to learn about the clients and programs they represent.
4. Engage RFP reporting services to learn about RFPs as they are released.
5. Network with existing customers to discover other programs.
6. Use state and local government procurement websites to find recurring contracts.

Except for the first method which is almost always the best, these are not presented in any particular order. Some may represent better methods for you depending on the products you sell and the markets you sell into.

1. Keep and log every RFP you receive

One of the easiest ways to identify and track recurring programs—*and the future opportunities they represent*—is by saving and logging every RFP you receive.

Most recurring contracts awarded through an RFP process span about three years for the initial term, but they often include clauses that allow the buyer to extend the contract for one or two single-year terms without having to rebid the contract. After the three-, four-, or five-year term is concluded, though, the internal program manager is generally required—either by corporate rules or government regulations—to initiate a new procurement and issue a new RFP for the contract.

What this means is an RFP you receive today is for a current procurement. In a very real sense, though, it's also a lead. It's advance notice of a future procurement that will be initiated in the next three to five years. I know, I get it, this doesn't help you in the short term, today, but that's OK. In the world of formal procurements, you need to be taking a long-term view, anyway.

If you receive an RFP today, one you are neither expecting nor are prepared for, your chances of winning are low. The more expensive and strategically important the program is to the buyer, the more your chances decrease. Therefore, though my recommendation might change based on specific circumstances, I would *generally* advise one of my clients against bidding on an RFP they get today if they aren't prepared for it.

However, I would also encourage them to view today's RFP as notification about a future opportunity. I would urge them to begin preparing for when the RFP goes back out to bid in three, four, or five years.

2. Building target profiles

Another excellent way to find contracts is to build an ideal customer profile. The idea is simple; if you are successful with a specific segment in a particular market, start calling on other companies who operate in that same segment of that same market. Here's an example.

Suppose you review your customer base and determine, after careful analysis, you are most successful selling your product to construction companies who build hospitals and employ over 350 people. As a salesperson, I'd do some more work to find out why you've been successful in that market and segment, but then I'd go looking for other construction companies that fit the same profile.

Suppose you sell K-12 school administration software. After analyzing your existing customer base, you immediately recognize your biggest success comes from smaller, rural school districts with smaller budgets and fewer internal IT resources. This is your sweet spot. Own it.

Knowing where you do well is a great place to begin looking for new opportunities.

3. Building relationships with industry consultants

Consultants can sometimes play a major role in procurements, but their involvement is usually specific to particular industries. For example, I've encountered consultants more frequently where employee benefits are involved such as health insurance or retirement benefits.

If you work in an industry where consultants are active in the procurement process, it's important you identify who they are *and* the clients they represent. Moreover, it's important you build relationships and establish your credibility with them. It's important because, while consultants don't generally make the final decision for the buyers they represent, they do have influence, and sometimes a lot of influence.

Working with consultants is frustrating to a lot of sellers who view them as little more than obstacles that unnecessarily weasel their way in between buyers and sellers—an additional level of bureaucracy that adds little or no value but lots of extra work. As frustrating as it may be, though, buyers view these consultants as adding value. Therefore, building good and positive relationships with consultants is a prerequisite to success.

There are a number of implications to this complex relationship, but the most fundamental is this; you aren't just selling to a buyer, and you aren't just selling to a consultant. You are selling to both a buyer and a consultant. Therefore, you can't just build relationships with buyers and hope you're going to be successful. Likewise, you can't just build relationships with consultants and hope you're going to be successful. You won't often win if you don't have relationships with both, and you can't build relationships with both unless you first identify both.

Recognizing this, there are a few different ways to identify consultants. First, if you're in an industry where consultants are prominent, you probably already know who many of them are because you're already getting RFPs from them for the buyers they represent.

The second way to identify consultants is to do an Internet search for the kinds of services you sell. Consultants are interested in selling their services to the same organizations you're also targeting. So pretend to be a buyer, and then search on words or terms you might use if you're trying to find the services your company provides. A list of consultants will undoubtedly pop up.

4. RFP reporting services

There are a number of companies today that offer notification or listing services when an RFP is issued from federal or state agencies. Sellers can subscribe to these services for a fee.

I have a love/hate relationship with these services. If a seller uses these services to find newly issued RFPs with the intent of writing a proposal in response, I don't like them. For all the reasons we've been discussing so far, you can't just find an RFP, write a proposal in response, and reasonably expect you have a good chance at winning the business. Sure, you may win one in twenty, but that means you have to engage your staff to write twenty proposals in pursuit of one. And the one you win may not even be a good fit for what you do.

However, if a seller uses these RFP notification services as a prospecting technique to find new, future contracts they weren't previously aware of, to learn about contracts so they can be prepared when they are released in three years' time, I love them. Provided you don't try to respond to the current RFP, this is an effective way to identify contracts that you can pursue in the future when they are rebid.

5. Working with existing customers (for internal and external referrals)

Every experienced, professional salesperson will attest that one of the greatest ways to find new sales opportunities is to seek referrals from existing customers.

Suppose you sell administration software for schools, and you've got a very happy customer with the ABC Fictional School District. Bob Jones is the superintendent at ABC, and he attends all of the regional and national school administration seminars and conventions. Over the last 20 years, Bob has gotten to know pretty much everyone in the field. As a salesperson, I'd be spending time strengthening my relationship with Bob and finding ways to encourage Bob to introduce me to other school districts who would be able to use our administrative software.

That's one example. Here's another.

Suppose you have a happy customer with the Ohio division of XYZ Office Copier Corporation. Sally Jones is the head of that division. As a salesperson, I'd be talking with Sally to see if she would consider introducing me to the company's divisions in Indiana, Michigan, Kentucky, West Virginia, and Pennsylvania—all the states surrounding Ohio. Or maybe I'd see if she could introduce me to her boss who oversees each division across all 50 states.

The point is this: if you have a happy customer, and the person you know is in some way influential within his or her universe, take time to explore whether they would be willing to help you network to others within that universe.

6. Use state and local government procurement websites to find recurring contracts

The really great thing about state and local government procurement programs is they broadcast what they're going to be buying. The first step is to find your state's procurement website and sign up. They'll ask some questions including what kinds of services you sell. If they issue an RFP for the type of service you sell, you'll be included on the list of vendors who receive the RFP.

But the other thing you can do, which is far better, is to search on past RFPs that relate to the services you sell. Once you find these RFPs, you will be able to identify recurring programs, sometimes the program managers who oversee them, and what kinds of specific services they required in the program. This will give your sales team the opportunity to start calling on and building relationships with program managers long before the next RFP is released.

RESEARCHING CONTRACTS

At this point in the process, you've identified a bunch of recurring contracts but you may not know much about them. For example, you learned ACME Fictional Coffee Cups periodically goes out to bid for payroll services, but you may not know much more. So before you start contacting people and making phone calls, you might benefit by investing a little time researching the programs you found. The good news is this may be far easier than it sounds, and it's all thanks to the procurement officer.

Getting help from procurement officers

Procurement officers are generally willing to work with vendors *if they think it means another person bidding on a project.* Before we proceed, let's pause for a moment and explore why this is.

Procurement staff and contracting officers are tasked, among other things, with ensuring procurements are competitive. When an RFP is issued, the procurement officer must be certain at least X number of vendors respond. If they don't get at least that participation rate, some buyers will cancel the procurement citing lack of competition. This is so important that sometimes, contracting officers are incentivized to reach certain levels of competition. At the very least, their efforts are frowned on if they cannot come up with enough vendors to make the procurement sufficiently competitive.

Recognizing what motivates them, you can often get what you want (information) by appealing to what they want (a competitive procurement). More to the point, I'm suggesting if you contact a procurement officer and dangle a carrot in front of them, you can often get information that might otherwise be more difficult to acquire. Here's an example of how I might approach a procurement officer named Bob:

> *"Hi Bob, I understand you have a contract that periodically goes out to bid for uniform services. Our two organizations haven't worked together before, but this is something we might be interested in bidding on. I'd like to ask you a few questions."*

Often this simple introduction is all that is necessary to begin a conversation and gather basic information about the contract. If Bob believes he is talking with an interested vendor, he may be willing to share information in the hopes he'll convince you to participate in the next bid.

Procurement people like Bob are no different than you or me or any other salesperson; we're all selling something. It's just instead of a product or service, Bob is selling 'why you should participate in their procurement.'

Recognizing that Bob is motivated to 'make a sale,' you need to be ready with a set of questions. Following are relatively basic questions I *might* lead with when speaking with a procurement person like Bob.

- Tell me about the program. What services are you buying?
- Can I get a copy of the previous RFP you issued for this?
- When do you expect it will next go out to bid?
- Every company is different. How do you folks handle procurements? Do you have one decision maker or do you convene a committee to review proposals?

If Bob is helpful and accommodating, I will likely press with some more in-depth questions.

- Who is your current vendor?
- How long have they had the contract? Is this their first term or have they been managing it for a while?
- The word "on the street" is your staff is happy with your current vendor. I know it's important to go out to bid periodically, but if your staff is happy with the current vendor, what would it take for them to consider another vendor?
- Can I get a copy of the proposal that ABC company submitted—the one that helped them win the previous bid?
- Who is your program manager internally?
- How do you choose who will be on the selection committee?

These are just examples of questions I might ask. Depending on the industry I'm in or the product I'm selling, the questions will change. Depending on the demeanor of the contracting officer I'm talking with, I may ask more questions or fewer. Regardless, I'm going to get as much information as I can before I get shut down.

Information to collect

The preceding list of questions alludes to it, but as you research each contract, there is important information you should try to collect. Listed here is the most important of the important.

1. Relevant contract dates

There are multiple dates that are typically associated with a recurring contract. What I want to know most are the current contract dates and, in particular, the date the next procurement is scheduled to be released.

- **Current contract dates.** I'd like to know when the contract was last awarded, how long it's for, and when it is due to be completed.
- **Next procurement.** I'd like to know when they expect the next RFP to be issued. I usually don't get more precise than the year and quarter (ex. Q1 of 2026). You can get more specific if you want, but RFP release dates are notorious for getting moved around and especially pushed back. A general time frame is usually sufficient.

If you know these dates, then you know how much time you have before the next RFP is issued. This gives you the opportunity to begin planning your sales campaign.

2. Copies of past RFPs

Having a copy of the previous RFP is an excellent way to quickly understand the scope of the program, the particular specifications they identified as important, recurring topics or themes that explain what this buyer finds most important, etc. And as we've discussed, most procurement managers will gladly provide this if they believe it will lead to another bidder for their next RFP.

It's not always possible, but having access to earlier RFPs in addition to the most recent is even better because it provides "storyline perspective;" it lets you see how their interests have changed over time. This is important.

RFPs have themes just like all good proposals have themes. If their primary concern in the initial RFP was a lower price, but their primary concern in the subsequent RFP was vendor responsiveness, this indicates their interests changed. As a salesperson, I would want to know all about their changing interests. This helps me to understand their motivations more clearly, which is fundamental and foundational to their current decision-making process.

3. Copies of competitive proposals

Successful sellers take the time to build competitive dossiers on other vendors. A competitive dossier may include information gathered from public sources such as the competitor's website, product brochures, or online review sites. It might also include intelligence from private sources such as debriefs with former their employees or interviews with their former customers.

One of the best sources of competitive information, though, is having access to a sales proposal written by your competitor. In their zeal to win the business, sellers will often share lots of relevant information, including how they are positioning their product, their perceived strengths over their competitors, the names and backgrounds of their subject matter expert staff, and more. It's often amazing how much you can learn.

So how do you get copies of competitor's proposals?

Most government agencies are required by law or regulation to provide you with copies of proposals as long as you follow their posted process when making the request. And just to be clear, you do not have to participate in a particular procurement to be allowed to request proposals associated with a particular procurement.

- **Federal agencies.** The executive branch of the federal government is required by law to provide this information through the Freedom of Information Act (FOIA). All you have to do is use their established procedure to make the request and get their proposals.
- **SLED (state/local government and education) agencies.** Most state and local governments are also required to provide this kind of information through their own "Sunshine" or "Open Meeting" laws. The process for requesting documents varies by state, but it's easy to find if you look.
- **Commercial organizations.** Businesses are not bound by these laws and may refuse to provide this information to you.

If you are researching a B2B procurement, it's still possible to get copies of proposals from competing vendors. All you have to do is find a state procurement involving that vendor and then make an open meeting request for the proposals they submitted. It's not the same procurement, of course, but if it's the same product, you may still learn something.

4. The current vendor

It's always helpful to identify the vendor who is managing the current contract. Sometimes, that's hard to do because buyers don't want to share too much information about current operations with prospective vendors. Still, if you can find out, it's good information to have. If you know who you're competing with, and if you've been good at building competitive dossiers, you have a better idea how to position yourself in the next procurement.

If you can, it's also good to know how long the buyer has been working with the incumbent vendor. If the buyer seems to switch vendors every time the contract is rebid, maybe they haven't found a vendor they're happy with. If the buyer has been with the same vendor for the last 20 years, maybe they're set in their ways and unseating the incumbent is going to be nearly impossible.

In the end, anything you can learn about the incumbent, and the buyer's relationship with the incumbent, is helpful.

EXPAND YOUR UNIVERSE OF OPPORTUNITIES

Everything we've discussed so far has been about prospecting for recurring programs that already exist. This is relatively easy to do because, since the programs already exist, all you have to do is find them. Still, this isn't your only avenue to develop new business opportunities.

Enterprising salespeople understand they can expand their universe of opportunities by seeking out potential buyers who do not currently use what they sell.

Unlike recurring programs that already exist, this approach is more arduous because it requires you first convince someone they need what you're selling, and then convince them you're the best company to fulfill the need. It requires more work.

If you're successful, though, this proactive approach to creating new opportunities has many advantages.

1. If your product is innovative and unique, or you are the only vendor who offers anything like it, any procurement that results will likely be skewed in your favor. In some cases, you may even be able to arrange a sole-source procurement.

2. Even if other vendors are able to offer the same or similar services, you were the first who brought it to the buyer's attention. This gives you an advantage to frame the conversation and influence any procurement that results.

Despite the extra time and effort this approach requires, you've created a new procurement opportunity that you are presumably well-qualified to win, and likely better positioned to win than most other vendors who might pursue it.

PROSPECTING FOR CONTACTS

So far, you've compiled a list of programs that appear to be a good fit for what you're selling, and you've done enough research to collect some basic information about each. Well done!

Now it's time to begin doing what salespeople do so well — finding and meeting the decision makers and influencers who manage the programs you've identified. There are many great books and training programs that explore how to prospect for contacts, and most veteran sellers are experienced with this, anyway.

Still, here are a few tips I've discovered that are specific to formal procurements that might help you as you search for the right people to connect with.

1. Ask the procurement officer for an introduction

Procurement people are generally not the decision makers; they're the referees who make sure internal staff and external vendors are all following the rules of the procurement. It's the actual program managers or program management team who make the decision and select the winning vendor.

If you make contact with a procurement person, and they're helpful, ask if they will introduce you to the program manager. Frame it carefully.

Explain you only want 10 or 15 minutes for an introductory call and then you'll follow up by providing information about your product. The less risky and time consuming your request, the more likely they'll help.

There's always the possibility they'll say no, but if they agree, you'll be saving yourself a lot of time in your efforts to find the right person.

2. Search competitive materials for contacts

Many of your competitors are eager to share references and quotes provided by their customers. They're so eager because these quotes make them look good. In the process, though, they're inadvertently broadcasting some of their best contacts to their competition, including you.

Take advantage of this free information and use it. Contact the person they list. I understand the person being quoted is recommending your competitor, so you're probably wondering if they really are the best person to contact. The answer is yes.

Circumstances change. A happy customer today may be a disgruntled customer tomorrow. Indeed, when sellers get a good customer quote, they tend to use it repeatedly for a long time. The person who said good things about your competitor three years ago might have a different attitude today. I have personally found many great contacts that turned into customers using this technique.

When searching for these customer quotes and references, you should peruse the competitor's website, any brochures they publish, copies of proposals they submitted in response to RFPs, etc.

4.

Prospecting for One-Time Projects and Acquisitions

In the previous chapter, we discussed prospecting for recurring programs, and how they are relatively easy to find because they already exist and are rebid on a fairly regular basis.

Procurements associated with projects and one-time acquisitions are different. Unlike recurring programs that already exist, project-type procurements—constructing a new building, developing a new app, or buying equipment to outfit a new factory—don't exist before the procurement is launched. And since they don't exist, they can't be found.

Prospecting strategy: projects vs. programs

The strategy to find recurring programs is simple; find the program. It already exists so it is findable.

The strategy to find one-time projects is more complex. Since you can't find the project (because it doesn't yet exist), you have to find the decision makers and organizations who will one day launch a project or acquisition for the type of product or service you sell. This is a little bit more involved.

Many sellers who pursue these kinds of projects do not take the time to build relationships beforehand. Many wait for an RFP to get published and then they hustle to respond. This is a mistake.

With these kinds of projects, building relationships with potential buyers—beforehand—is essential. It's essential because most buyers will not award an important project to a vendor they do not know. Especially for procurements that are mission critical, expensive, or have a lot of visibility, there's just too much at risk. Therefore, when faced with choosing a vendor, most buyers will only award projects to, or buy products from, vendors with whom they have established relationships.

Clearly, this is a big challenge for sellers. If a buyer doesn't know them beforehand, doesn't have an established relationship, the seller's chances of winning the project are low. Really low. Single digits low.

To be seriously considered when a new project is launched, sellers need to find a way to establish themselves—*beforehand*—with the buyers and decision makers who will one day launch those projects.

Connecting with buyers

So how do you connect with buyers ahead of time, before a one-time procurement even exists? There are two ways to do it.

The first way is to build your brand in the market. In chapter 6, *Building Your Brand and Reputation in the Market,* we are going to discuss how to make sure they know you even if you don't know them. In project-focused markets, this is critical.

The second way, that we discuss in this chapter, is to identify the most likely buyers in your target market and then begin building relationships with them. The more buyers you know, the better they know you, the more likely you'll be brought into projects in the pre-launch phase. This is what you want.

BUILDING ONE-TO-ONE BUYER RELATIONSHIPS

It's always best if you have a first hand, one-to-one relationship with the buyer before the RFP is issued. Even more preferable is if you have a *Trusted Advisor* type of relationship as described in the book of the same name by Maister, Green, and Galford. It's not enough to be an expert in your field, if you want to be an advisor who qualifies as "trusted," and benefit from all the perks that come with that, it is essential that you earn your buyer's confidence that what you recommend is both good advice and in their best interest.

Before you can build that trusted relationship, though, you need to find them and get to know them. That's what this chapter is about.

1. Focus on buyers in specific target markets

The best place to look for potential buyers is to focus on the target markets you already serve.

- If you are a construction company that builds school buildings, you need to assign a salesperson to get acquainted with all of the buyers in all of the school districts within your region.
- If you build roads, you need to assign a salesperson to get acquainted with all of the state and local government buyers within your region. You should probably assign another salesperson to target all of the commercial and residential builders who build parking lots or residential streets.
- If you are a staffing agency, and you specialize in sourcing nurses who themselves specialize in particular disciplines, you need to get acquainted with all of the HR professionals at local hospitals who hire those specialists.

You already know the target markets where you operate and have a track record. It's critical you network and develop relationships with as many people in those target market as you can.

2. Build an ideal buyer profile

Targeting specific markets is ideal, but sometimes, it takes more effort to find the specific decision makers within each market. One of the best tools to help you do this is to create an ideal buyer profile.

It's a simple idea. Analyze your existing customer base, identify where you've been most effective, summarize the traits those customers have in common, and then compile those traits into an ideal profile. Now use that profile to guide your prospecting efforts.

If you sell proposal automation software, for example, chances are you have sold to businesses across many markets (federal, state and local government, commercial) and many market verticals (construction, staffing, IT networking, app development, etc.). When you analyze your customer base, though, you might say, "hey look, we've had most of our success with this vertical, in this market, under these circumstances."

Figure out *where* you do well, figure out *why* you do well there, and then start calling on other companies that match that profile.

3. Network among existing contacts

Another great way to find prospective buyers is to network with your existing contacts. In the business world, people in similar roles will frequently get to know each other, meet formally or informally to discuss shared challenges, discuss existential threats, learn about innovations and best practices, and more. This happens across many professional groups:

- Primary school administrators within a city or region.
- High school administrators within a city or region.
- College presidents among other similar-sized colleges.
- Facilities managers at hospitals, hotels, and schools.
- Finance managers and controllers in service industries.
- Benefits managers for municipalities, cities, and other local governments.

These connections can be through shared professional organizations or industry groups, or they can be more personal connections between two people who used to work together. Regardless, these interpersonal relationships can be gold mines for salespeople networking through a professional community.

If you have a good relationship with a buyer, if they are satisfied with your product or service, ask them if they would be willing to introduce you to their associates at other organizations. These kinds of personal introductions often result in some of the best prospective buyers you'll find.

4. Read industry news

For organizations that pursue project-oriented contracts, like construction projects, browsing local news sources and newspapers, and staying involved with current events, is often one of the best ways to determine what projects are coming down the road.

- If you are a commercial construction company, and the local hospital has gone on record saying they're running out of capacity, this might be a potential new project. Now might be a good time to get to know the people at the hospital.
- If you build roads, and a local township has announced plans to launch a five-year road improvement project, you probably want to get to know the council members or the engineer for that township.

For major capital improvement or infrastructure projects, news sources can be an excellent way to determine what's to come.

Phase 2:
Pre-RFP Selling

The pre-RFP Selling phase can be organized into four parts:
- Building your brand—making sure they know about you even before you first meet.
- Discovery—learning about them and their needs.
- Education—teaching them about you and your capabilities.
- Solution building and discovery wrap-up—making a plan to make the sale.

5.

Pre-RFP Selling: The Big Picture

The selling process associated with formal procurements is unique from most other types of procurements, and one of the biggest differences is its length. When pursuing a strategically important opportunity, I always advise salespeople to begin their selling effort at least 12 to 24 months before the RFP is published.

Many sellers are dubious when they hear this. Compared to other B2B sales processes that are days or weeks, months at most, they have difficulty understanding how a sales process can last so long.

I understand their hesitancy. I once thought the same way. So let's begin by answering the question: "Why does pre-RFP selling take so long?"

WHY PRE-RFP SELLING TAKES SO LONG

Procurements that involve RFPs are usually expensive, mission critical, high-profile, or some combination. With so much at stake, the people overseeing procurements want to make good decisions that are in the best interest of their organizations.

Of all the different techniques buyers use to improve decision quality, minimizing or eliminating uncertainty is one of the most effective. The more effectively they eliminate uncertainty, the more likely they'll get the outcomes they want.

Minimizing uncertainty

For buyers, the best way to avoid uncertainty is to become familiar with the vendors who will be bidding on their project. If they know the seller well enough, they know what to expect if and when they formalize a relationship. Conversely, if they do not know the buyer well enough, they don't really know how any subsequent relationship is going to develop. At that point, all they're doing is hoping a productive relationship will result.

This is precisely why most buyers with strategically important projects or programs are *unlikely* to choose vendors they do not know well; it introduces far too much uncertainty into the procurement decision.

The salesperson's dilemma

While it is true buyers will not choose you if they don't know you, it is also true they don't go out of their way to get to know you ahead of time. This is understandable. Most buyers are busy running the current program and doing their day jobs. Learning about vendors for a procurement that won't be formally launched for another couple years is just not on their radar.

This is the dilemma you face:
1. Buyers won't consider you if they don't know you.
2. Buyers are not motivated to get to know you ahead of time.

The salesperson's singular mission

If you want buyers to get to know you well enough to consider awarding you their business, it's on you—the salesperson—to initiate, foster, and cultivate the relationship.

This necessarily means salespeople have to be proactive. They have to find the decision makers, initiate the relationships, and develop them to the point where the buyer feels comfortable awarding a strategic project to the seller.

So, to answer the question that started this discussion, this is why the selling process spans at least 12 to 24 months. It's because it takes that long to establish relationships, build familiarity, communicate capabilities, establish credibility, and do all of the other things that qualify you in the eyes of the buyer.

SALES STRATEGY: THE BIG PICTURE

When pursuing formal procurements, a salesperson's objectives change over time. Initially, 24 months before the RFP comes out, your objective is to make buyers aware of you and your company. As the pre-RFP selling process progresses, your objective is to engage the principals, to learn more about them and their program and their people, and to help them learn about you. As the RFP publish date gets closer, your objective is to transition into a more focused effort to understand their issues and challenges and to propose solutions that would address them.

The point is you aren't selling solutions on day one. It's too soon for that and they'll shut you down. Even though they aren't actively interested in talking with vendors about their program, you can still use this early, pre-RFP window to expand awareness about you and your company. Later, when you start engaging them more regularly, they'll recognize you. They'll see you aren't just a fly-by-night operator but someone who is established in their market, a legitimate contender, and someone they should consider as they prepare for the next procurement.

Selling in formal procurements is a marathon, not a sprint. Take care to run the entire race, pace yourself, and you'll be rewarded by being well positioned when the RFP, the proverbial final sprint, is published.

6.

Building Your Brand and Reputation in the Market

As a professional seller, I study elements of psychology to better understand topics like persuasion and how people make decisions. It helps me be a more effective salesperson. One of the many topics I've found helpful in my studies is something called the familiarity principle.

The familiarity principle says people tend to think more favorably towards things (or people) they recognize. Translated into everyday terms, if there are two boxes of cereal on the shelf, and you've heard of one but not the other, you are more likely to pick up the box you recognize.

I am not a social psychologist, and my pithy explanation risks oversimplification, but it seems clear the familiarity principle applies well to the work salespeople do when pursuing formal procurements. If there are two proposals on your desk, and one of the proposals is from a firm you recognize, you are more likely to favor their proposal versus the other proposal from the firm you've never encountered before.

Buyer familiarity matters

There are two reasons buyer familiarity is important for salespeople. First, if you are prospecting and trying to arrange an initial call with a potential buyer, and if they've heard of you or your company, they may be more willing to take your call and begin a conversation. This isn't going to win you the deal, of course, but it might be enough to get your foot in the door. That's not nothing.

The other reason familiarity is important is because, no matter how hard you try, you will not get to know every prospective buyer or find every prospective opportunity beforehand. As a result, you may not learn about some opportunities before the RFP is released. In general, this is disqualifying. But if the buyer is at least familiar with your firm, and the solution you are proposing is a super good fit for what they need, you may still have a chance—slim though it may be—at winning their business.

Is brand building a marketing or selling function?

Whenever we discuss building your brand, most sellers immediately think it's a function of the marketing department. While the marketing department clearly has an important role in building your company brand at a market level, what I'm talking about in this chapter is something more personal.

I am advocating that the salesperson builds a personal brand for themselves, and for their company by association, and become the de facto face of their company to the buyers in that market.

So how do you do that?

The best way to build buyer familiarity is also the most obvious; involve or even immerse yourself and your company into the market or markets you are pursuing.

INVOLVE YOURSELF IN INDUSTRY ASSOCIATIONS

Many industries form professional associations. These associations give their members opportunities to network with other professionals, agree on best practices, share insights, provide training, earn certifications, and more. Listed here is a representative sample.

- Marketing professionals have the American Marketing Association (AMA).
- Marketing professionals in the construction industry have the Society for Marketing Professional Services® (SMPS).
- Legal professionals have the American Bar Association® (ABA).

- Relocation professionals have Worldwide ERC® (WERC).
- Proposal professionals have The Association of Proposal Management Professionals (APMP).

For salespeople, these associations represent marvelous opportunities to build your brand and reputation in the market. This is because they've already done the hard work; they created one place most of your potential buyers congregate.

Begin with local chapters

If markets you target have associations, and you aren't already involved, volunteering with local chapters is a good place to begin. Non-profit associations are always in need of volunteers, so they will surely appreciate your offer.

Once you begin showing up at meetings and events, you will quickly identify the volunteer opportunities that are available—*and that will provide you the most exposure.* Pick one you like and get started.

Sponsor events

Associations are always looking for sponsors to cover the costs of local meetings, networking events, training events, etc. These sponsorship opportunities are generally not very expensive at the local level, but they're a great way to begin getting your name out and win exposure for your company.

Provide meeting space

If your organization has ample meeting space, you may consider offering your facilities to host monthly meetings or periodic events. This is a win-win for everyone. Not only are you providing the association with meeting space at no cost, there's a big benefit to having potential clients visit your offices. It's a great way to foster familiarity.

Speak at meetings and tradeshows

Professional associations are always interested in delivering educational programs and presentations to their members. It's one way they provide value. The challenge they face, though, is continually finding new programming to deliver.

You can be a valuable resources to these associations, and build your reputation among buyers, by arranging for your internal SMEs to deliver presentations or participate as expert panelists during conventions, symposiums, and meetings.

These presentations are helpful to associations because it gives them more programming to provide their members, to attendees who learn something new they can apply in their work, and to the vendor who delivers the presentation and wins lots of exposure.

Advice: start small

One thing I learned providing presentations to professional associations is to build a great presentation for a popular topic but then deliver it for a chapter or local venue. Engage participants in order to gain as much feedback as possible and then revise your presentation to make it better. After that, ask chapter leaders if they would like to see the presentation delivered at one of the association's regional or national meetings. By then, you'll have practice delivering it, it will be refined with audience feedback, and you'll have local leadership recommending it to the national team.

Contribute articles (ask what they want)

Many associations have newsletters they publish monthly or quarterly. The newsletter staff, who are often volunteers, usually struggle to develop new content. Investigate what kinds of articles they usually publish, and then consult with your team to draft a list of articles to propose to their editorial staff.

If they choose one or more of your articles, you will benefit from the wider exposure you'll get. You'll be establishing your expertise and fostering familiarity at the same time.

Advertise on websites and in publications

This may be something you coordinate with your marketing department. If you identify opportunities to advertise in association newsletters or chapter websites, it might be an effective way to promote familiarity. Repetition is great for familiarity; the more they see your name and your company's name, the better for you.

Acceptable behavior

One of the important things to remember is you can't be in "product pitch mode" all the time. Associations are a great way to network and make new connections, establish your credibility, and build familiarity. Make your involvement about that. If you launch into a sales pitch every time you meet someone new, you're going to alienate everyone.

This does not mean you have to stop being a salesperson. It's just you have to do it the right way. Take time to get to know people, and give them time to know you. Set up display tables at events so people can reach out to you if they want whatever you sell.

If you get involved with associations, you'll definitely get a reputation. Make it a good one.

COLLABORATE WITH AFFILIATE VENDORS

When you are working to build your reputation in a market, one technique is to associate or collaborate with affiliate vendors. In this context, an affiliate vendor is a company that sells to the same clientele you do, but they aren't in competition with you. For example, you sell training services to CPA firms. An affiliate vendor might sell accounting software to CPA firms.

Depending on your industry, it can sometimes make sense to collaborate with affiliates to host programs, presentations, or other events. You both get more exposure, you are seen collaborating with other recognizable names in your field, and all that helps to promote familiarity.

This isn't a good option in every circumstance, but if it is for you, it can be a great way to get in front of and build familiarity with buyers.

INDUSTRY MAGAZINES

If your industry is large enough to have trade magazines or other online media, consider contributing educational articles written by your SMEs on topics of interest to the publication's readership. Most editors have the same challenges associations have; they have to create a lot of content to fill the pages of their publications.

One of the best ways to approach this is to assemble a few ideas about articles or even columns you are prepared to write. Then contact the editor and see if they'd be interested in collaborating.

Being published in a trade publication is a great way to establish your expertise and build your brand.

Resource to other writers

Trade publications like articles that reference industry experts. One effective but often overlooked technique to get more exposure for your firm is to make your internal experts available to a publication's writers as experts. This way, someone else is writing the article and doing all the hard work, but they quote your expert and your company gets exposure.

The familiarity principle is a salesperson's best friend. Embrace it.

7.

Pre-RFP Selling Part 1: Learning About Them

Professional salespeople are already familiar with discovery. It's where you meet with the buyers and influencers, ask questions, uncover problems, get to know individual buyers, build rapport, establish the credibility of your team, and more.

Discovery is always important, but it's especially important where formal procurements are involved. That's because once an RFP is issued, and sometimes in the period just before it's issued, buyers prohibit all conversation between seller and buyer. In other words, if you don't learn everything you need to learn before the RFP is issued, you probably aren't going to learn it after.

The rest of this chapter discusses the various things you want to discover about the buyer during the discovery phase.

DOCUMENT THE PROGRAM OR PROJECT

This sounds fairly straightforward and for the most part it is. It's important to understand the buyer's project or program in all its intricacies. Dig deep, learn everything you can. You probably do this already.

Because of the nature of formal procurements, though, there are a couple additional tasks to include in your discovery effort.

Get multiple perspectives from multiple people

Don't limit your inquiry to only one person. If you sell a health benefits plan, don't limit your conversations to just their benefits manager. You must also talk with other people who are involved in the program. In addition to the benefits manager, for example, you may also talk with union leaders, or arrange meetings with individual employees who you discover are educated about, and well-versed in, issues related to health benefits.

The more connections you make, the more you learn from each person, the more targeted and effective your proposed solution will be.

Get the backstory

Most organizations have at least some experience with the type of product or service they are procuring. In other words, they've got history. Your job is to understand that history.

If you're a construction company working with a school district, find out how their previous building projects have gone.

- Were they happy? Frustrated?
- Did those projects come in on time and on budget, or late and over budget?
- What did they learn?
- Which delivery methods do they prefer? Design-build? At risk? Are they happy with the approach they used?
- How has their approach to building evolved over time?

This is just one example, but hopefully you're seeing the point. It's not enough to know what they want today; it's important you know what's gotten them to this point.

The more you learn about their backstory, what they've already done, what they've already experienced and learned, the better positioned you will be to propose a solution that is both in their best interest and aligned with their thinking.

IDENTIFY AND GET TO KNOW ALL OF THE DECISION MAKERS

Veteran salespeople already understand the importance of identifying and getting to know the decision makers as well as the people who influence the decision makers. This requirement is *even more important* in formal procurements, and that's for two reasons; more people are involved in formal procurement decisions, and conversations are prohibited after RFPs are published.

1. More people are involved in formal procurement decisions

One reason organizations use formal procurements is because they want more involvement from more staff in the decision-making process. They don't want the VP of Finance deciding, in a vacuum, which vendor should handle employee retirement accounts. They want the people who will be using the services to also be involved in choosing the provider. It's all about involvement and inclusion.

> Organizations use formal procurements because they want more involvement from more staff in the decision-making process.

For salespeople, this means it's not enough to identify and build a relationship with the ultimate decision maker. You must also identify all of the influencers who are involved, have strong opinions, and have the leverage to sway others' opinions. Then you need to meet them, get to know them, and build rapport with them.

** Include your SMEs and operations staff **

Identifying and meeting with decision makers and influencers is important, but it's critical that you also take your internal experts, your SMEs, to meet with theirs. We discussed this in an earlier chapter on process design considerations so there's no need to restate it all here. Still, it's important to emphasize that buyers want to meet your SMEs and operations staff—the same people who will be managing and delivering the services they receive. The more meetings between your staff and theirs, the better off you'll be.

The bottom line is you and your SMEs must identify and interact with *all* of the decision makers and decision influencers throughout the buyer's organization, not just the "top dog" who signs on the dotted line.

2. Conversations are prohibited after RFPs are published

The second reason it's so important to identify all of the decision makers, beforehand, is because most organizations prohibit interaction between sellers and buyers once an RFP is issued. Some even prohibit interaction when an RFP is imminent. If you get an RFP, and you haven't built a relationship prior, you aren't going to learn much more going forward.

I openly admit that I have talked with some salespeople over the years who dismiss this. They say—and they aren't lying—that they have reached out to buyers and demanded that, before they agree to respond to an RFP, they must be granted access to decision makers so they can learn more about the opportunity. Here's my response.

First, no state or local government agency would accommodate this demand because if they did, and it became known, every other bidder would have grounds to protest the award if that vendor won. Further, the protest would be upheld on review by administrative review or in court. Therefore, most state or local government procurement people presented with this demand would just chuckle and dismiss you.

Second, it is possible you could get away with this when pursuing a procurement from another business, but so what? Even if you are granted an audience with the decision makers, you are still entering the marathon during the last 100 yards while the other vendors have been participating for the previous 26 miles. Do you really, honestly think you have a chance at making up that much ground when you entered the race at the very end? Don't be naïve.

This is not to say this approach has never worked because it has, just not consistently. And this goes back to the main point: do you want to win every once in a while, or do you want to build a more consistent, reliable stream of business?

Dave's rule: don't run the final 100-yard sprint if you haven't first run the 26-mile marathon.

What about procurement officers? What's their role?

Many salespeople misunderstand the role procurement officers play in the procurement process. Procurement staff are generally not decision makers. In most cases, procurement people are more like referees; they make sure the players follow the rules of the game, but it's the players on the field who ultimately decide who wins.

So while procurement staff can disqualify vendors who don't meet minimum qualifications or who violate procurement rules, it's generally the line managers and organizational staff that decides who wins the business.

I'm making this point because I often speak with salespeople who argue they have been working with a buying contact when in actuality, they're only working with a procurement person. The procurement person is a good person to know, to be sure, but most of the time they aren't the decision maker.

This is an important point. If the procurement person is not a decision maker, but they're the only person you've talked with, you aren't ready.

The bottom line is if you want to sell effectively, consistently, you must identify and interact with all of the decision makers and buying influencers in an organization. Do that and you'll start winning more consistently. Don't and you won't.

DOCUMENT BUYER REQUIREMENTS, OBJECTIVES, __AND__ THE MOTIVATIONS THAT PROMPTED THEM

Documenting buyer requirements seems, at first glance, an obvious thing to do. But doing it well requires a lot of investigation into their objectives and requirements, and especially the motivations that prompted them.

Documenting requirements and objectives

When an RFP is published, it lists requirements or specifications to which all vendors must comply. The requirements are accompanied by language like "the vendor will..." and "the vendor shall..." Subject matter experts and proposal writers are then responsible for ensuring their solutions and proposals comply with the list of requirements the buyer mandates.

> It's important to understand the requirements that appear in an RFP are a lot like icebergs; what you see is only a fraction of what's there.

I love this analogy because it's so fitting. The story behind the requirement often goes deep, just like the iceberg. The good news is, during this pre-RFP discovery phase, salespeople have ample opportunity to not only identify each requirement but to also uncover the whole story behind them. This is important.

A university wants to build a new student center and they are emphasizing student safety. That's what the RFP requirements says. But it would be a lot more helpful if you knew that during the previous project, some students snuck onto the construction site and one was seriously hurt.

Knowing the backstory will help you to configure a better solution that more effectively addresses the client's needs. It will also help your proposal team to draft a much better storyline when it's time to articulate how your solution is going to solve their problem.

Document individual motivations

In a previous chapter, we discussed at length how every requirement or specification that appears in an RFP originates from a person. Whatever happened that prompted it, someone thought it important enough to get it included as a requirement in the RFP. Here's the important part.

The people who publish RFPs don't want to share all of their problems with the world, at least not in stark terms. So cautious procurement staff start with the concern that was raised and then they sanitize it into an organizational requirement that's appropriate and safe to share with the world. Emphasis is on the word "sanitize."

- The university is OK saying they want a safe worksite. They are less enthusiastic admitting one of their students was hurt at a job site.
- A hospital is OK saying candidate backgrounds will be thoroughly evaluated. They are less enthusiastic sharing that a previous staff doctor they hired didn't actually have a medical license.

See the point? The requirement as it appears in an RFP is sufficiently sanitized to exclude the backstory, but knowing the motivation that prompted it will help you to both create a better solution and address their concerns more effectively. I cannot emphasize this enough—if you want to sell well, you must understand the personal motivations of the decision makers and influencers.

WHY ARE THEY GOING OUT TO BID NOW?

Buying organizations are generally resistant to changing vendors, and that's for good reason! Changing a vendor is both a lot of work and a lot of risk.

Changing vendors is a lot of work

Buyers are generally resistant to change vendors because, for many, changing from one to another is an involved and challenging process that impacts many parts of their organization. The accounting department has to implement new invoicing and payment protocols, compliance has to ensure the new vendor meets applicable regulations, legal has to review and negotiate new contracts, program staff has to coordinate reporting and operational procedures, and more. Different programs have different challenges, but changing a vendor is generally an involved and time-consuming process.

Changing vendors is risky

In addition to the time and effort involved, there is always a risk the new vendor will perform poorly. Imagine being an internal program manager that endures all of the administrative headaches associated with switching vendors, and then the new vendor turns out to be no better or even less effective than the vendor they replaced. Not a pretty picture.

Why do buyers ever go out to bid?

If switching vendors is so difficult and risky, why would a buyer ever go out to bid? Ultimately, there are only two answers. Buyers go out to bid because they have to or because they want to. Each has important implications sellers need to understand.

Going out to bid because they have to

For recurring programs, most state and local government organizations and many commercial organizations are required to go out to bid about every three to five years. In other words, the internal people responsible for managing the program have no real choice in the matter. This is important to understand.

Sally is the program manager, and she is very happy with their current vendor. She's also very busy. She doesn't have enough time in her day to get lunch much less bring on a new vendor. But she goes out to bid anyway—not because she wants to but because she has to.

Going out to bid because they want to

The other reason a buying organization goes out to bid is because, despite the time, effort, and risk, they *want* to. In general, there are five reasons why buyers *want* to go out to bid.

1. **Management change.** When I am the competition selling against an incumbent, a change in management is one of my favorite scenarios. That's because when a new manager comes in, they frequently want to "change things up." When this happens, it is often a threat to the incumbent, but it opens the door to the competition. Good for you if you are the competition, not so much if you're the incumbent.

2. **Significant change to program requirements.** It's difficult or sometimes even contractually impossible to ask an existing contractor to significantly change their program in the middle of a

contract. So when an internal program's requirements change significantly, most buyers will issue a new RFP. This is an opportunity for competing vendors because, in a sense, there is no incumbent vendor for the newly published specifications. The existing vendor still has an advantage, but the door is opened a crack.

3. **Economic conditions change**. After the recession began in the US in 2008, a number of buyers issued new RFPs—sometimes before the existing contract term ended—because they were getting internal pressure to cut costs. When a buyer goes to bid early for this reason, it's an opportunity for competitive firms, but only if they're willing and able to get aggressive on pricing.

4. **Current vendor is falling short**. If you learn that a buyer is going to bid out of dissatisfaction with their current contractor, you've got a legitimate opportunity. It's not definite they're going to change from their current vendor; they may just be using the RFP as a way to shake them up or get some new performance guarantees. Still, the buyer is at least open to a new vendor with a good story to tell.

5. **To squeeze the current vendor for a better deal**. Sometimes, buyers will go out to bid with no intention of changing vendors; they just want to negotiate a better deal with their current vendor. There's no better way to conduct a negotiation than when the negotiation is accompanied by competitive pressure, so they use your organization for no other reason than to negotiate a better deal with their current vendor.

There are other reasons buyers want to go out to bid, but these five are the scenarios I've encounter most frequently.

Why is all of this important?

If you're serious about winning more of the RFPs you bid on, you must understand why a buyer is going out to bid.

If the buyer is going out to bid because they have to, not because they want to, how likely are they to change vendors with all the risk it entails? It's certainly possible to unseat an incumbent vendor, but it's just as likely they're only going through the motions. Their mission is to get the procurement done as quickly and efficiently as possible, then choose the same vendor they already have and get back to the hundred other items on their priority to-do list.

On the other hand, if you pursue procurements where the buyer is going out to bid because they want to, your chances of winning improve.

You need to figure out which it is.

DOCUMENT THEIR DECISION MODEL AND CRITERIA

There is no single method that buyers use to select a vendor. Indeed, organizations have unique requirements and therefore create unique selection methods that they believe are most likely to get them the outcome they want.

The challenge for salespeople is to identify the type of selection process the buyer is using. Not only do you want to reflect their process in your efforts, you should be structuring your efforts so you can capitalize on, and get the most benefit from, the selection process they've chosen.

I've so far made the case to work with the operations managers and staff, not procurement staff, because they are the people who make and influence purchase decisions. In this case, though, the procurement people can be very helpful in tutoring you on how they will be making the purchase decision for a particular procurement.

Common selection methods

There is no universal list of procurement selection methods, but the following is a good representation of some of the more common methods you'll find among state and local government and commercial buyers.

Lowest price technically acceptable (LPTA)

For products or services that are considered to be more of a commodity, procurement departments often use an approach commonly referred to as LPTA, or lowest price technically acceptable. The way it works is a contracting officer is assigned to review your proposal and determine if it is technically acceptable. Technically acceptable means it meets the minimum qualifications. Of those that are acceptable, the proposal with the lowest price wins.

This approach only works well if the product or service being acquired is a commodity. Sadly, many local governments use it too often for services that are not really commodities.

A committee assigns points

Another popular method involves assigning a committee of people to review your proposal and assign points for each item, and then the points are added up. The vendor with the most points wins. There are variations on this method, but it is a common approach with many state and local government agencies.

A committee makes recommendations to a decision maker

Most often used in commercial organizations, this approach involves a committee of experts reviewing the proposals and then making recommendations to a board or an individual decision maker. That person or board considers the committee's recommendation and then makes the purchase decision unilaterally.

Proposal sections are assigned by expertise

Most often used in commercial organizations, this approach involves distributing each section of the proposal to an internal subject matter expert for their review. The internal IT expert, for example, reviews the section of the proposal specific to IT. Each of these experts then assesses vendor capability and makes recommendations to a board or an individual decision maker, who then makes the purchase decision.

Match your selling process to their buying process

The point of this discussion is not only to enlighten you about the variety of selection methods that buyers employ, but also to ensure the selling process you create has a mechanism to capture this information and share it among the business development team.

This is so important because the selection method the buyer uses will likely dictate your pre-RFP selling approach and later, how you write your proposal. For example, if you know the buyer will use the 'lowest price technically acceptable' (LPTA) method to select a vendor, it's generally a waste of time to sell quality or innovation or long-term cost savings. That's because in this scenario, all they care about is whether you are compliant with their requirements, and among those who are, which of you has the lowest price.

In contrast to the LPTA method, if you know they are going to be assigning sections to subject matter experts, it makes sense during the pre-RFP selling phase to get your subject matter experts talking and interacting with their subject matter experts. This will allow their experts to gain familiarity with what you offer, to learn about and address their technical concerns, and in general, to demonstrate the superiority of your solution long before the RFP is issued.

HOW IMPORTANT IS PRICE?

I've heard many salespeople claim "the only reason buyers issue RFPs is because they want the lowest price." In fact, any salesperson who articulates this obsolete generality is being both irresponsible and shortsighted. It's irresponsible because price is almost never the only thing buyers consider when purchasing anything.

In the real world, the importance of price will vary depending on the unique goals of each procurement. In some procurements, price is the primary selection criterion. There are other procurements, though, that have different objectives.

I remember one recent procurement where the buyer was willing to spend far more if the vendor could produce better outcomes for their user base. To them, it wasn't about price; it was about results. They wanted better results, and they were willing to pay for them.

Every buyer is different just as every procurement is different. If you're going to be effective at winning more of them, you must understand how important price is in their selection process. You need to understand it because it influences your entire selling strategy.

8.

Pre-RFP Selling Part 2: Educating Them About You

The discovery process is a two-way street; it's not just you learning about them, they want to learn about you, too. The previous chapter discusses you learning about them. This chapter discusses the part of discovery where they are learning about you. It explores the many methods and tools you can use to help them learn about you, your product, and your team.

To be clear, I discuss each of these two discovery functions separately to give each the attention it deserves. In real life, the two happen simultaneously.

Your objectives during discovery

From a seller's perspective, this part of discovery requires that you accomplish two important objectives; educating buyers about who you are and what you do, and establishing your credibility.

Objective #1. Educating buyers about you

Perhaps the most fundamental objective of the discovery process is also the most obvious; you need to educate your buyers about you, your company, the product you sell, and your staff who implement, service, and support it.

Objective #2. Establishing credibility

Before a buyer awards a major contract to a vendor, they want to know the buyer is credible, is able to deliver everything they promise. This means they not only want to evaluate the product or service you provide but also your experience in the market, the people on your staff who deliver it or manage it, the infrastructure you've implemented that supports it, and more.

They want to know you're real and you're credible, you'll deliver what you promise, and you'll be around tomorrow to support it.

GETTING IN FRONT OF BUYERS—FACE-TO-FACE MEETINGS

One of the best ways to get to know buyers is to meet them face to face. This is nothing new to veteran salespeople; getting a meeting with "the decision maker" is, initially at least, your primary objective. It's where you interact with the person (or people) who make decisions AND has budget authority—the holy grail of buying contacts. This initial meeting is where you talk about their program, understand their objectives, and identify their pain points. It's also where you introduce them to your company, your experts, your products, and how you can help them accomplish their objectives.

Getting a meeting with the decision maker and/or decision making team is an important first step to launch your pre-RFP selling effort. But recognize it's just that, a launch point, a great first step. The second step is to identify and meet with all of the other decision makers and influencers who are involved in or will influence the purchase decision.

This is important.

I've made the point multiple times throughout this book that what counts is not just the singular relationships between the salesperson and the decision maker, what matters just as much are all of the interpersonal relationships you build between your experts and theirs. The more relationships you foster between your two organizations—the more your people know them and their people know you—the better off you'll be.

With that in mind, enterprising salespeople should use the initial meeting to identify the other decision makers or influencers you need to contact. Consider these examples.

> Salesperson: "An important aspect of this program is providing you with accurate monthly invoicing. Our billing manager has built a great system to generate invoices with line item explanations. Is there a person in your accounting department he can speak with to ask a few questions about how you prefer your invoices to be formatted?"

Here's another.

> Salesperson: "Protecting your customer's personal information is critical. We've implemented an array of data security and physical plant measures to harden our service against unauthorized access. To ensure our systems meet your requirements, I'd like to schedule 15 minutes between our security officer and your compliance officer to ensure we have all of the systems in place.

It's not just the salesperson talking with the decision maker, it's subject matter experts talking with subject matter experts. This approach offers lots of benefits.

Not only are you ensuring you know what they're going to be asking for when the RFP is released, you're fostering familiarity and new relationships. When the buyer's compliance officer reads your proposal, they will be more likely to say, "*I remember Sally from ABC company. She is the only vendor who called to ask me about our security requirements.*"

In a competitive procurement, recognition and familiarity is vital.

STAYING IN FRONT OF BUYERS—SELLING TOOLS

Learning is a process. Especially in a world with so many distractions, it often takes time and repeated exposure to the same or similar messages before communication actually occurs. This DOES NOT mean you should spam buyers until they consign you to the junk folder. It does mean you should find ways to stay in front of prospective buyers—repeatedly, over time, and through different methods and channels—to ensure the message you are trying to communicate is actually getting through to the recipients.

This effort requires that you produce a myriad of selling tools— documents, videos, webinars, seminars, and more—to help you stay in front of buyers and increase the chances of your message getting through.

In this section, we're going to discuss four topics:
- Types of selling media
- Topic categories
- Guidelines when creating selling tools
- Making a plan and pacing your delivery

1. Types of selling media

In this context, selling tools are defined as different types of media your salespeople share with buyers at various stages throughout the pre-RFP selling process. Listed here are the most common types of media sellers may use.

Documents

The nice thing about documents is how relatively easy they are to produce and share. Once created, they can be produced as PDFs and shared by email or made available for downloads. They can also be printed for distribution at tradeshows, during site visits, or via postal delivery.

I understand that many younger people prefer videos or podcasts instead of more traditional brochures. But understand that many older buyers still prefer to hold and read a hardcopy—and have the flexibility to quickly scan through the document—rather than be subjected to watching a video or webinar.

Videos

Videos can be an effective way to communicate a message. When producing them, though, be sure to highlight your senior-level subject matter experts and frontline operations staff. The more you give these talented, knowledgeable people the opportunity to share their insights and wisdom, to shine, the more buyers will think favorably about your company. It's also an excellent way to demonstrate the depth of your staff.

This is an important point. Salespeople in formal procurement environments should strive to showcase their professional operations and SME staff whenever they can, and videos are a great way to do that. These professionals are often your best salespeople.

Webinars

The Covid pandemic taught sellers how to use webinars to continue interacting with potential buyers even if we couldn't be with them in person. The good news is we stayed connected. The bad news is we all began suffering from webinar burnout. It was a classic case of 'too much of a good thing is a bad thing.'

This does not mean all webinars are bad, though. In fact, webinars can still be great selling tools, but only if we learn from our past experiences and figure out how to use them well.

So what have we learned?

I learned the best webinars are short and to the point. Instead of an hour-long session that covers a lot of topics, it's preferable to create a 15 minute webinar focused on just one. A buyer may not have time in their day to watch an hour-long presentation, but could easily find 15 minutes to learn about a topic they care about.

The more narrowly you can define webinar topics, and the shorter and more to the point you can make them, the more people will be interested in watching.

Podcasts

Podcasts can also be a very popular method of providing relevant information and staying in front of buyers. Many people love listening to podcasts, especially when they're commuting or traveling.

Like webinars, though, I recommend defining the topic narrowly, keeping them relatively short, and getting to the point quickly.

Blog posts

I'm a huge fan of blog posts. I find these posts are a great way to both establish credibility and build your brand among buyers in the markets you target.

I maintain a list of topics I want to write about based on what I think buyers want to learn about. I find inspiration by listening to the questions new customers most frequently ask. I also invest time reading LinkedIn® posts regularly and paying attention to the questions people ask, the comments they make, and the challenges they're struggling with.

From this list, I create a library of articles that are organized into three folders:

- In development
- Ready to publish
- Already published

I always have a handful of articles ready to publish, but I usually never publish more than one or two a week. I use this metered approach because it lets me stay in front of buyers without overwhelming them by posting too many articles in too short a time.

Once the article is published in a blog, it becomes a selling tool. All I have to do is send a new customer a link to blog articles they are interested in knowing about.

2. Topic categories

Depending on where you are in the selling process and what the buyer is interested in at that time, there are many different categories of topics you can discuss.

Product-specific feature highlights

I know we live in a world where salespeople want to talk about solutions, but buyers also want to know about the product you sell. They aren't necessarily at the solution stage yet; they're still learning about all of their options.

Suppose you want to buy a pickup truck, and someone asks you, "What kinds of options do you want?" Personally, I'd respond with, "I don't know because I haven't bought a truck in a while. I don't know what options are available." The point is, buyers can't really formulate their needs until they fully understand what options are available to them.

As you identify your selling tool topics, be sure to include topics that discuss the important features, functionality, or methods that are, or might be, most relevant to buyers.

Product-specific frequently asked questions

Frequently asked questions (FAQ) documents can be a great way to educate buyers about your product. The questions you ask and answer should, in general, be based around what buyers ask most often, but there are two additional things to keep in mind as you plan what FAQs to create.

First, make your FAQ documents topic specific. If you usually hear lots of questions around implementation, build an FAQ that discusses all of the implementation questions you typically get. If you hear a lot of questions about support, create another FAQ about your support program, how quickly your team responds, escalation procedures, etc.

Second, make sure you include questions that highlight those things that make your product different and better than the competition. If you are able to complete the implementation in two days, but it takes a week for your competitors, be sure to include a question in your FAQ that highlights this advantage.

Popular industry topics

As a young salesperson who began my selling career before the Internet was a thing, I remember getting questions from buyers not just about my products but also about what was happening in the industry. Things were happening, trends were evolving, and without the Internet to inform them, buyers were thirsty for knowledge. They anticipated, in my role as an industry salesperson, I could offer the insights they sought.

Today, buyers still want to understand what's happening in the industry, but it's a different kind of challenge. In contrast to the pre-

Internet age marked by a drought of timely information, today's buyers are overwhelmed with lots and lots information from lots and lots of sources, and not all of it in agreement. Buyers today don't need more information, they need help interpreting the informational onslaught they face.

In this environment, buyers are again looking to sellers, but this time, it's to help them make sense of everything they're seeing and reading. Here are the kinds of questions they're asking:

- This new law was just passed. What does it mean to our business?
- Ohio and Kentucky just passed conflicting regulations on the same topic. How do we navigate that?
- There's a new protocol that was just published to protect consumer information. What does this mean for small retailers?

You get the idea. Figure out the important industry topics your buyers care about, create insightful pieces to address their concerns, and you'll go a long way to become a valuable and credible resource to them.

Customer case studies

Case studies are one of the best selling tools available to salespeople, but also one of the most underutilized. To be clear, I am not talking about the kinds of case studies they used to give us in college; lengthy, overly-detailed, multi-page monstrosities that induced sleep better than prescription pharmaceuticals.

I am talking about case studies that are short; no more than three or four paragraphs. They should also be limited to a single theme, a single topic, that is clear and easy to understand.

Invest in customer case studies. It's a great way to use your past successes to attract new buyers.

Company background abstracts

Company backgrounders can be great selling tools, but only if done correctly. Here's what I mean.

Most company backgrounders and company histories are long-winded dissertations that drone on about when you were founded, how long you've been in business, how many offices you have, the awards you've won, etc. These types of backgrounders are almost universally self-centered, boring, and nobody wants to read them.

Instead of these long-winded bloviations, consider writing a succinct backgrounder that talks only about your involvement in a particular market segment. If you're a construction company that builds university campuses, for example, write a backgrounder that highlights your involvement with local colleges. Be sure to discuss your expertise managing the things universities care about most, like constructing new buildings without interrupting ongoing campus life, ensuring job site safety despite being surrounded by wild and crazy college students who might not always use their best judgement, etc.

The same construction company might draft another unique company backgrounder describing their experience building jails and correction facilities, how their experience can influence designs to better ensure inmate and guard safety, how no prisoners have ever escaped during one of your projects, and more.

Do you see the point? If you write a generic company backgrounder that discusses your history and experience building all kinds of buildings, so what? Nobody cares. But if you share your experience building the same type of building this particular buyer is interested in, you're accomplishing lots of goals at once. You not only have one more tool to use to stay in front of buyers over the course of a long sales process, you're establishing your credibility and expertise in the particular discipline they care most about.

3. Guidelines when creating selling tools

Over the years, I've learned many lessons about selling. One of the best is also one of the simplest: "you don't have to say everything, you just have to say what's important." Say what's important, and then stop talking.

If you want to create selling tools that appeal to buyers, there are two important ideas that should guide your efforts; define topics narrowly, and create multiple selling tools for each topic so they are customized to each unique market segment you are pursuing. Let's explore.

Define topics narrowly

Have you ever done research on the Internet because you wanted to know one thing, but the pages you visit won't tell you that one thing until they talk about lots of other things, first? It's very frustrating.

If you want your selling tools to be effective, focus on one narrowly defined topic at a time. Here are some examples.

- Instead of a lengthy brochure titled something like, "How to Write Proposals in Response to RFPs," narrow your topic to something more specific like, "How to Write Customer References that Influence Buyers."

- Instead of a long video titled something like, "How to Build Maximum Security Prisons," consider something more specific like, "Designing Prisons to Promote Officer Safety."

- Instead of an hour-long podcast discussing "Everything You Ever Wanted to Know About School Administration Software," consider something more targeted like, "Ensuring Student Record Security in Online Administration Software," or "How Online SaaS Systems Minimize Local School Administrative Burdens."

People are busy. They are much more likely to carve out 15 minutes of their day to read a short brochure or listen to a brief video. But if you try to tell them everything, all at once, they'll probably miss most of it or tune out entirely.

If you want your selling tools to be effective, stick with one, narrowly-defined topic at a time.

Draft each topic for unique market segments

Most buyers are not interested in learning about something not specific to their needs. The more focused a selling tool is to a particular market segment, the more relevant it will be to those buyers. If you're a business owner buying a pickup truck to transport big, burly workers, do you want to read a brochure that highlights family adventures where the main focus is pulling boats? It might be the same or similar product—a pickup truck—but it's a different clientele and therefore a different message. Target the message to the clientele.

Suppose you represent a construction company and you've invested a lot of time and effort creating methods and disciplines to construct buildings on busy campuses without disturbing ongoing operations. A narrowly defined topic like this is great, but narrow it even further by drafting one version for medical campuses, another for prisons, and a third for university campuses. Here are some examples.

- Draft a brochure unique to hospitals. Explain how you create signage and routing so visitors not familiar with the facility will find their way to their destination without getting lost in a maze of construction-related detours.

- Draft another brochure unique to prisons. Explain how you build security plans that segregate prison populations from construction activity, account for all construction equipment that could be repurposed for nefarious use, and contingency plans if a security issue occurs.

- Draft a third brochure unique to university campuses. Explain how you coordinate with their athletic programs to avoid loud or obstructive work during major athletic events, build dedicated construction access roads to avoid traffic snarls, etc.

You're selling the same idea to each market segment—your ability to construct a new building without disturbing ongoing operations—but you're tailoring the message so it's relevant to each.

4. Making a plan and pacing your delivery

As a rookie salesperson, one of the biggest mistakes I made when starting a new customer relationship was sharing everything I had—*all at once*. The only tools I had at that time were documents, but I'd fill an envelope with every document and send them all together.

I came to learn, with time and experience, this method was terribly ineffective. In my youthful exuberance, I thought I was increasing my chances of making more sales by sending more stuff. In fact, I was shooting myself in the foot because I was sharing too much too quickly. It's hard to take a sip from a firehose, but I didn't appreciate that.

Early in the selling process, when you identify a particular buyer, take the time to make a plan about how to stay in front of that particular buyer. You need to figure it out for yourself, but here is a realistic example protocol to get you started.

- **Arrange an initial meeting.** Learn the specific things this buyer cares about. Write those things down and rank them by their perceived importance.

- **Follow up with your first selling tool.** After your initial meeting, provide the buyer with the selling tool that addresses the biggest issue or concern they articulated in your initial call. "In our meeting today, you said you were interested in customer service response times. Here's a document that..."

- **Create a timeline.** Using the list of items this buyer cares about, identify the additional sales tools you want to send, along with a timeline for sending them. Be sure to pace yourself with appropriately spaced intervals between contact.

- **Work your timeline.** Be true to the timeline you create. At the appropriate time, reach out to the buyer and remind them about your original call. "Hi Bob, in our call last month, you said you wanted your staff to have access to experts who could advise them. We produced this short, ten-minute video, that explains how we do precisely this."

- **Include periodic phone calls.** It's really easy to fall back on emails instead of one-to-one verbal interactions, but recognize it's important for you to speak to buyers periodically. This will help you gauge their interest and demeanor. Do they like you? Do they not like you? Are they guarded, or are they somewhere in the middle? Those are things you cannot learn through emails.

Remember, in addition to establishing your credibility, your objective is to stay in front of them over time, building familiarity and giving them ample opportunity to get to know you and your company. And you do that by pacing your interactions with them.

Obviously, if the pre-RFP selling effort is shorter—if you found the opportunity later rather than earlier—then you have to share more information sooner and more frequently. Still, try not to share everything all at once. Trying to take a sip from a fire hose never works.

Target the right buyers with the relevant message

You are busy. So are your buyers. Don't waste their time with topics that are not relevant to them.

Suppose you're selling an employee benefits program to an organization. By this point, you should have lots of different types of selling tools to share with different kinds of buyers. Just make sure you send the relevant document to each person.

- Data security is important to everyone, but the head of the union is probably more concerned about responsive customer service to their members.
- Responsive customer service is important to everyone, but the VP of IT is probably more concerned with the specifics of your data security systems.

See the point? You only get so much time and attention from any single buyer. Don't waste it by sending them stuff that is irrelevant to them.

WARNING: DON'T TALK ABOUT SOLUTIONS TOO EARLY

Salespeople are fond of talking about solutions, and that's a good thing. In fact, it's a great thing. It represents an evolutionary advance from the old days when salespeople were little more than a legion of professional product peddlers and feature preachers.

Today's modern legion of enlightened salespeople understand the distinction between products and solutions. Instead of just peddling products, we build custom solutions configured to address each buyer's unique needs. We may be selling the exact same office copier to each buyer, for example, but we configure each solution with various feature, payment, service, and support options to make it is compliant to what each buyer needs. We aren't selling products, anymore, we're selling solutions to problems.

Despite this evolutionary advance in our profession, there's a tendency among sellers to begin talking about solutions far too early in the selling process, even before they've figured out the scope of the problems and challenges the customer faces. This unfortunate tendency undermines their credibility because it suggests the seller isn't really proposing a unique solution, they're just peddling products but calling them solutions.

Don't start talking about solutions too soon.

So as unconventional as this advice might sound, at this early point in the process, it's OK to talk about your products.

Before you climb back up to your product peddling pulpit, though, this does not give salespeople permission to revert to the old days where all we did was preach features to potential buyers. That didn't work before and it still doesn't work today.

What it does mean is this. As you learn about different problems or challenges the buyer faces and is trying to solve, reference a feature or function of your product that addresses their problem. You may talk about how you've helped others solve the same problem, and you could provide the buyer with a brochure or a link to a video that discusses that feature.

Buyer: We've been struggling with our current office copiers. They're high maintenance, which is becoming very expensive, and we've had to replace them more frequently than we'd like.

Salesperson: Actually, we hear this same concern a lot from customers across the market. That's why we went back to the drawing board and redesigned our copiers with a reverse phase plutomatic core.

It's brand-new tech but, basically, it reduces the number of moving parts by half. This doubles the service life of the copier while at the same time cutting maintenance costs by

> two thirds. When I get back to the office, I'll send you a PDF that describes this feature in more depth, and how some of our other customers have been able to reduce maintenance visits and costs, and extend their copier's life.

See the point? You're still focused on the benefit they get, the outcome they'll receive, but you aren't proposing a solution just yet because you don't know the totality of their problem. And you're certainly not regressing to a fire hose presentation mentality where you blast them with a bulleted list of 250 features, 247 of which they don't care about. Through the give and take of discovery, you are addressing specific features within the context of specific problems they're trying to solve.

9.

Pre-RFP Selling Part 3: Wrap-up and Recommendations

At this point in the process, you're about six months before the RFP is released. If you've been faithfully following the process, you and your SMEs have spent the last 12-18 months meeting with buyers, getting to know them and their needs, giving them the opportunity to meet you and your expert staff, establishing your organizational credibility, and more. Well done! It's been a lot of hard work, but you've positioned yourself well for this final stretch before the RFP is released.

Now stop. Take a deep breath.

This is the point in the process when you and your team need to refocus on the big picture and assess where you are in your pursuit effort. This is where you ask the important questions about what you know, what you still need to learn, and what you still need to do.

It's those last two—'what you still need to learn' and 'what you still need to do'—that are so important. There are a thousand pieces to this puzzle. It's far better to realize you're missing an important puzzle piece today versus after the RFP comes out.

This section explores how to approach this critical wrap-up phase.

DISCOVERY STATUS MEETING

Schedule a discovery status meeting with your entire business development team. This includes any operations or SME staff who have been involved in meeting with buyers, any decision makers who will have to authorize expenditures or investments, any pricing people who will need to structure a price quote, any HR people wo will need to figure out how to staff the new project or program, and anyone else who should be involved.

This meeting might ultimately involve a wide cast of characters, but if the opportunity looks promising and sufficiently lucrative, it's probably worthwhile to include all the relevant people who will be meaningfully involved in the effort.

In this meeting, the first order of business is to ask and answer three important questions:
1.   What do you know?
2.   What do you not know and still need to learn?
3.   What are the big tasks you still need to address?

Some sellers might dismiss this as 'extra work' or 'just one more unnecessary meeting.' They're wrong.

When you are pursuing a major project, one your company really needs to win, investing in this meeting is critical. It gives your team an opportunity to learn and share. Most important, it gives them a chance to collaborate, to "think out loud together."

This is vitally important. You are the salesperson who is tasked with bringing the deal to fruition, but the people around the table are those who will actually deliver whatever solution you propose. They are the experts. Listen to them and give them a chance to contribute.

1. What do you know?

Prepare a briefing that consolidates the most relevant facts and circumstances that you and your team have learned through your pre-RFP discovery efforts. You need to structure this briefing in a way that works best for your team based on how involved they've been. If the relevant members were involved over the last 18 months, you can be brief, just sharing the highlights. If the relevant members haven't been deeply involved, a more thorough review is necessary to bring everyone up to speed.

Encourage your team to speak up if there's anything you left out. It is not uncommon to learn a team member was talking with a buyer, learned something important, but in the pace of daily life, neglected to share it with your team. Now is the time to encourage them to speak up.

2. What do you not know and still need to learn?

As a veteran of many procurements, there are few things as frustrating as getting an RFP and only then realizing there was a requirement or objective or something you did not previously understand or fully comprehend.

First, share your own list of the things you feel like you should know but don't. Second, task your team to help you complete the list. You might say something like this:

Team, we want to do our best to minimize any surprises after the RFP comes out. What do we still need to learn?

Do we fully understand all of the important requirements related to this procurement? Have we identified all of the buyers? Do we know where they stand?

If there are things we don't know or you suspect we don't know, please share it now. But even after you leave this meeting, please keep thinking about this question. If you come up with something, please get back to me in the next couple days with anything we might need to explore further.

Now's the time to get it right.

Encourage your associates to step up. Some of them may have some reservations here or there about this or that, but for whatever reason, they may hesitate to come forward. Make it easy for them to come forward. The more potential issues you identify now, the better off you'll be later.

3. What do you still need to do to prepare for the RFP?

By this point in your selling effort, the scope of the buyer's project should be clear. Moreover, you should have a really good idea about all of the different things it's going to take to win their business.

Now is the perfect time to plan ahead and start making the necessary preparations and investments—such as buying needed equipment, hiring necessary staff, collecting important statistics—that you know will be required to satisfy their requirements.

It's likely you've been thinking about some of these things already, but now's the time to start making decisions and plans.

Equipment

Some projects require you have certain equipment or capabilities to comply with RFP requirements. If you have those things, great. If you don't, now may be the perfect time to acquire them or make arrangements to acquire them.

It's ideal if you can procure them after you win the business, saving you from investing in something before even knowing if you're going to get the contract. Sometimes, though, you have to invest in these things ahead of time or you will not satisfy their minimum requirements at the time the RFP is released.

- A construction company, for example, might need to procure an onsite concrete plant to satisfy the requirements of a project.
- An audit company might need to acquire new servers to accommodate the buyer's larger than normal data feed.
- A service company might need to open a new office in order to satisfy the buyer's requirement that all vendors be local.

Decide what you need, when you need it, and make all the necessary plans so you are ready.

Certifications or qualifications

Depending on the type of product you sell, a buyer may require that you meet established industry standards or earn specific certifications before they'll contract with you. If you haven't already, now might be a good time to begin seeking these certifications.

- A software development company that has access to consumer credit information may need multiple layers of security systems and a high-level security certification.
- An insurance audit company that handles PHI, or Protected Health Information, may need a certification that demonstrates they have the security measures and organizational policies in place to appropriately handle and process personal health data.

Earning certifications can take time, sometimes a lot of time. The sooner you start doing the work, the more likely you'll be ready when the RFP is released.

Staff and expertise

Depending on the type of project you are pursuing, the buyer may require you to have certain experts, either already on staff or committed to join your staff, if you are awarded the business. If you have these people on staff today, great! If not, you need to start looking now so you'll be ready when the RFP is published.

Clearly, finding highly qualified people is challenging, and the more qualified they are, the more challenging the task. Beginning your search for the right professionals now, while you still have time, is essential.

Subcontractors and suppliers

Depending on the product or service you sell, you may rely on subcontractors and suppliers to deliver the final product. Buyers may require you to have mission critical subcontractor relationships in place ahead of time, before being awarded the contract.

Regardless of the procurement requirements, you should vet your third-party relationships—ahead of time—so you are confident they can provide the services the contract requires and the service levels you expect.

Evidence and proof

Buyers are generally unwilling to accept the claims sellers make in their proposals unless those claims are accompanied by proof, evidence, or documentation.

- You claim your software is 30% faster? That's great, it would really save us some time. Prove it and I'm interested.

- You claim you can fill staffing positions faster than other agencies and with better-qualified applicants? Marvelous, that would solve so many problems for us. Prove you do this regularly and I'm interested.

- You claim your office copier is 30% more reliable requiring 50% fewer maintenance calls? Woohoo, that would save us a lot of time and money! Prove it's true and you have a new customer.

Hopefully, you're getting the idea. Buyers are not willing to accept sellers' claims without some evidence corroborating the claim. This means sellers need to be ready to supply proof. If you already have the proof to support your claims, great! If not, you need to begin collecting it.

If you wait until you get an RFP to begin compiling proof, it might be too late. But if you start considering these things now, six months before the RFP comes out, you may still have time.

At this point in your meeting, you and your team have, hopefully, come to some consensus about what you know, what you still need to learn, and what major tasks you still have to accomplish. This is a good start.

WHAT RECOMMENDATIONS DO YOU WANT TO MAKE?

The next major topic of your meeting is to consider any recommendations you want make to the buyer as they work to formulate their project or program.

Take this effort seriously.

Buyers want to work with sellers who can help them make good decisions. They look to you as consultants, experts in your field, but they only want to work with people who have their best interests at heart. If they believe you have their best interests at heart, and you make good recommendations they recognize will benefit them, you've gone a long way towards establishing yourself as a credible expert and a trusted resource. The buyer will start looking to you for guidance. That's a big accomplishment.

The opposite is also true. If you make recommendations that do little more than position your product in a more favorable light, if you try to manipulate their RFP in your own selfish favor, they will recognize it and you will be undermining the credibility you've worked so hard to establish.

MAKE A TARGETED SELLING PLAN FOR THE NEXT FEW MONTHS

So far, you know what you know, you've identified what you still need to learn, you've identified the investments or initiatives you'll need to make to be ready when the RFP comes out, and you've decided on any recommendations you want to make to the buyer.

You've accomplished something else, too; your entire team has a shared understanding and vision about this opportunity. You're in a great spot.

Now, with all the intelligence you've acquired, your job is to make a plan. This planning involves two things:

1. You and your team need to make a specific list of tasks to accomplish before the RFP is released. This is the strategy part.
2. You need to assign those tasks to various team members, along with deadlines for completion. This is the administrative part.

It's important to get buy-in from all members of the team. It's not good if you have a plan but others aren't committed to it. Therefore, be sure to do two things. First, encourage each team member to reach out to you, offline if necessary, if there's something they're concerned about or not confident in. Some people are not comfortable speaking up in a larger forum, but if they know something you don't, you still want to hear from them.

Second, as the salesperson managing this disparate group, it's important you regularly follow up with each person who has been assigned a task. You're down to the wire, so there is less latitude if someone is not able—or does not appear able—to accomplish the assigned task. This is when you need to step in and figure out how to get it done.

Now your job is to go out and execute your plan.

APPRECIATE WHAT YOU'VE ACCOMPLISHED

You have so far made a really big investment in your pre-RFP selling effort, but look at how much you've accomplished. Seriously. All your work has put you in a great competitive position.

Remember that most other vendors have not been engaging the buyer so diligently. They haven't been meeting with decision makers and influencers, nor have they been establishing their credibility and expertise. Most of them are still sitting at their desks wondering when the RFP is going to drop.

While they know almost nothing about this opportunity, you know almost everything. Not only that, the buyer is familiar with you and your team.

This is a good place to be, and it's all because you decided to be proactive and make the commitment to do the work. Well done.

Phase 3:
Proposal Planning and Development

I said at the beginning this book is not about the writing part of the proposal process, it's about the selling part. But this does not absolve salespeople from being involved in the proposal development effort.

Even if you aren't writing proposal content, you still need to be involved in its planning and development. You still need to lead your team. This section explores how.

10.

Bid/No Bid Decision Making

To bid or not to bid, that is the question.

Salespeople are an optimistic bunch. They see an opportunity—any opportunity—and immediately think they can win it. To be clear, optimism is a good trait among salespeople. Faced with skeptical buyers who are perpetually on guard, usually cantankerous, and sometimes even hostile, it is a salesperson's optimism that often keeps them plugging along.

Still, a salesperson's unrestrained optimism is most effective if tempered with a healthy dose of realism. And just in case there's any doubt, here's the real: NO! You cannot win every opportunity you encounter. Just because you receive an RFP doesn't mean you have a chance at winning it.

If that's the real, here's why it's a deal: chasing every opportunity—and especially those you have little or no chance of winning—is expensive and wasteful. Indeed, using scarce organizational resources to pursue unqualified or poorly qualified opportunities, absent serious due process and consideration, borders on professional misconduct.

Yes, I understand saying those words, "professional misconduct," sounds severe. But never forget you have a fiduciary responsibility to your company to use resources wisely. Consuming them in pursuit of unwinnable opportunities is not using them wisely; it is wasteful and irresponsible.

Be proactive, not reactive

The solution? Don't be reactive when an RFP lands on your desk. Instead, commit yourself and your sales team to a formal, structured, methodical, and disciplined bid/no bid decision making process.

✖	Incorrect	"Hey! An RFP. Let's respond."
✔	Correct	"We just received the Acme RFP. We need to assemble the team and decide whether it makes sense to respond."

By committing your team to a methodical bid/no bid decision process, you are replacing knee-jerk reactions with disciplined decision making. In return, you will increase your win rate while minimizing both your workload and wasted resources.

Timing: when do you decide to bid or not bid?

Many sellers wait until they receive an RFP to begin their bid/no bid decision process. While common, there are many advantages to considering the bid/no-bid decision earlier in your selling effort, and then revisiting the decision multiple times along the way.

> The bid/no bid decision process works best if you begin at the early stages of the selling process, and then include multiple bid/no bid decision gates throughout.

Suppose you begin pursuing an audit services program in another state. Early in the discovery process, you learn the buyer will only consider vendors based in that state. Clearly, this requirement disqualifies your company from consideration, and therefore, it doesn't make sense to invest additional time pursuing it. Abandoning this pursuit early—long before the RFP is released—will save your business development team a lot of time they are now free to invest in other opportunities that have a better likelihood of success.

Considering the bid/no bid decision early is a great start, but I also recommend building multiple bid/no bid decision gates throughout your sales process. These can be as simple as a sales manager periodically meeting with each rep and asking a few pointed questions:

- Have you discovered any issues with the ACME Fictional Coffee Cups account?
- Any showstoppers?
- Any areas of concern?

The point is it doesn't have to be a major, time-consuming meeting, just a quick visit and someone asking the questions.

As the discovery process progresses, the questions asked at each decision gate should become more involved and include more of the in-depth questions discussed on the following pages. In other words, the farther you progress in the discovery process, the more rigorous your bid/no bid questioning should become.

If you're getting close to the RFP release, and there are still important questions you can't answer, that should tell you something. Pay attention.

Build your own bid/no bid process

Many larger organizations have exceptionally sophisticated bid/no bid decision support systems. Some of these systems are so sophisticated they calculate the probability you will win an opportunity—*and some even do it automatically!* Commonly referred to as "PWIN," the probability of winning seeks to inform decision makers about the likelihood they will win particular RFP opportunities.

While these sophisticated systems might be helpful to sellers that have the resources to build or buy them, many of the small and midsize sellers I've spent my career working with would be overwhelmed with such complexity. This is precisely why I recommend you create your own bid/no bid decision process so it is both right-sized for and well-configured to reflect the realities of your business.

In designing your process, it's important to include most or all of these six considerations:

1. Buyer familiarity
2. Requirements and capabilities
3. Competitive position
4. Production capacity
5. Proposal team capacity
6. Profitability

I've long believed the value of the bid/no bid decision process is not necessarily the answer you get (whether to bid or no bid), it's the deliberative process it forces your team to employ. It can save you from throwing good resources at bad opportunities, but it can also encourage you to invest more resources into borderline opportunities that just might produce the most profitable results. The process of asking and then working to answer the questions is often more insightful than the answers you get.

Whatever you do, just make certain the process you create is both right-sized for your business and workable. After all, it doesn't help having a process that nobody uses.

1. BUYER FAMILIARITY

In all my years as a professional salesperson and then a proposal writer, I've learned the ability to win sales opportunities requires far more than just configuring good solutions and writing compliant answers to RFP questions. Much of it, perhaps most of it, is about buyers and sellers getting to know and trust each other.

The interaction with the buyer—in the months and years before an RFP is released—is where you make the sale. The proposal you write in response to the RFP is where you close the deal. Remember this. Embrace this. Your success depends on it.

To that end, the first and most important part of any bid/no bid decision process is assessing buyer familiarity.

Do you have a relationship?

This is the single most important predictor of proposal success. Indeed, when designing a bid/no bid decision process, the existence of a previously-established buyer/seller relationship comes first, everything else comes second.

If I'm an HR manager choosing a benefits package for my company's employees, I will not rely solely on the words written on the pages of a proposal. There's too much at risk, especially since a good proposal writer can make even a lousy vendor look wonderful on paper.

I am going to rely, first and foremost, on the relationships I've built with the vendor staff I've met. I need to have confidence they know what they're doing, can configure a solution that actually solves my problem, and can ultimately deliver on the promises they make. A buyer cannot make those kinds of personal assessments about a seller based exclusively on the words in a proposal, it only comes through personal, one-to-one interactions. It only comes from getting to know people.

The proposal is important, to be sure; it lists the specifics, dots the i's, crosses the t's, and codifies the scope of the relationship. But none of those things matter if the buyer doesn't have confidence in the people who are submitting it.

If you do not have a previously-established relationship with the buyer, then your entire bid/no bid evaluation is based more on hopes and wishes than facts and predictable outcomes. Embrace that.

Do you know the decision makers?

Companies don't buy from companies, people buy from people. Most professional salespeople have heard this phrase uttered many times, and they've probably even reiterated those words, themselves. The sentiment is as true today as it's ever been, but it's especially true where expensive and complex business services are involved. Buyers need to know not just what they're buying, they need to know who they're buying from.

It's important to recognize, though, it's more than just the buyer getting to know the seller, it's also the seller getting to know the buyer. Decision makers have personal motivations, and it's those motivations that morph into RFP requirements. If all you know are the requirements written in the RFP, but not the motivations that prompted them, that's not enough. You don't know the all-important backstory. That's an issue because it's the all-important backstory that often gives you an edge over competing vendors. Consider the following example.

An RFP might ask how long you've been in business, request copies of financial statements, or request your organization's credit score. All of this may seem like routine requests included with many RFPs. But if you know the backstory—that the last two vendors managing their program couldn't finish the contract because they were struggling financially and losing staff—then you could do a much better job to craft your content so it more effectively addresses their real concerns. They don't care about your credit score, they want to know whether you're going to be around tomorrow.

You have to know the people so you can learn their motivations.

Do you know the influencers?

Everything we just discussed about decision makers applies to influencers, as well. The reason I list them separately is because too many salespeople too often ignore influencers while focusing all their attention on decision makers. This is a mistake.

In today's world, buyers value consensus and work hard to build consensus among teams. Everyone's opinions matter. Therefore, it makes sense for salespeople to learn the motivations and interests not only for the people who make the decisions but also for the people who influence the decision makers.

Do not neglect this group.

Do they like you?

This is so obvious that it doesn't need to be asked. Except it does.

There's an age old saying in the sales business that people buy from people they like. The corollary is also true; people generally don't buy from people they don't like.

Early in my selling career, I remember pursuing one opportunity that my company should have won. The buyer needed what we sold and their business name would have looked good on our corporate resume. Despite that, the decision maker didn't like me, personally. I don't know what I did, but I must have done something awful because she frowned whenever she saw me and was constantly saying sarcastic things directed my way. So instead of trying to force a bad relationship, I turned the opportunity over to an associate who got along well with that buyer. If I had continued on, my company would never have won the business. By turning the opportunity over to my associate, my company eventually won the business and my associate bought me a really nice dinner. Everybody wins.

Knowing whether a buyer likes you should be an intrinsic part of your bid/no bid decision making.

Do you know their history?

Buyers have history and you should know about it.
- A local school district preparing to construct a new classroom building has experience from the previous schools they've built. They have ideas about what works and what doesn't, what they like and what they don't, etc.
- A state agency that is rebidding their employee health insurance program has experience from the previous health insurers they've contracted. They have ideas about what works and what doesn't, what they like and what they don't, etc.

If you know them well enough to know their history—where they've done well, where they've fallen short, what they've tried, the lessons they've learned—you're likely in pretty good shape.

> In almost every procurement, the depth and quality of your relationship with the buyer is the most important predictor of your potential to win the opportunity. Bid/no bid decision making starts here.

2. REQUIREMENTS AND CAPABILITIES

An important part of making an effective bid/no bid decision is understanding the buyer's requirements and whether you have the capabilities to deliver the results they want.

Have you documented their requirements, and do you have the capabilities to provide what they want?

There's no sense bidding on a project if you can't deliver the goods. As part of your bid/no-bid decision process, therefore, it's important to assess your ability to deliver whatever the customer is buying.

- Do you have the infrastructure in place to deliver what they're buying?
- Do you have the staff you will need? If not, can you hire additional staff within the allotted timeframe?
- Do you have access to the contractors you'll need? To the equipment that is required?

It's OK if you don't have all of these things in the months and years before the RFP is released, as long as you identify what you will need and make a plan to get it.

Do you have performance data?

When it comes to major procurements, buyers will not take you at your word. Experienced sellers know they have to support all of the claims they make with facts, proof, and performance data. Do you have performance data you can reference?

It's OK if you don't have the proof you need in the months and years before the RFP is released, as long as you identify what you will need to make your case, and then make a plan to begin collecting it.

> **i** Your ability to deliver the product or service they are seeking—and prove you have the experience and ability to do it—is critical to your chances of success.

3. COMPETITIVE POSITION

Formal procurements are competitive—*by design*. Buyers want sellers to compete for their business because they know it will result in better outcomes for them. It could mean a better price, more services, better terms, or some combination.

Sellers have to go into every procurement knowing it's going to be competitive and then do their best to prepare for it by learning everything they can about the competitive landscape.

Do you know which vendors are competing?

Have you identified the vendors who will be competing for the buyer's business? You probably know most of them, already, but it's still good to confirm who is involved in this particular procurement.

When identifying competitive threats, be sure you also determine whether the buyer is considering keeping the program in-house. Sometimes, the most formidable competition is the buyer who is thinking about doing the work themselves.

Do the buyers appear to favor a vendor?

Sometimes, buyers have already decided the vendor they want to work with, so they tilt the procurement in that vendor's favor. If this happens in your favor, buy some champagne and party poppers because you're likely going to win. But if it's written in someone else's favor, consider no-bidding because you've probably already lost.

Do you know if the buyer intends to write the RFP to favor you? Or another vendor? If they have any predilections, you need to know what they are.

What are your competitors' strengths and weaknesses specific to this opportunity?

The key words in the preceding question are '*specific to this opportunity.*' The issue is not "what are your competitors' strengths in the market?" The issue is "what are your competitors' strengths in this particular opportunity?" The distinction is important because those are two different things. Consider this example.

Maybe your competitor has won numerous awards for hiring women and minorities. Good for them. That is a great accomplishment and something to tout in their marketing materials. The problem is today, ACME Fictional Coffee Cups is having severe supply chain issues. Within the context of their current procurement, ACME doesn't care about a vendor's efforts to promote women and minorities. All ACME wants to know is how each vendor is going to solve their supply chain issues. Supply chain comes first, everything else follows.

Turn it around. A particular vendor may do well in some circumstances but struggles in others. A vendor that has lots of support locations across the Eastern U.S., for example, may have an advantage supporting projects in that region. But if they're bidding on an opportunity on the West coast, the same vendor may struggle mightily.

The point of this question is to identify each competitors' strengths and weaknesses, advantages and vulnerabilities specific to this opportunity. Only then will you be better able to evaluate your chances of winning the business in a one-to-one competition.

What are your strengths and weaknesses specific to this opportunity?

In the same way your competitors have strengths and weaknesses, advantages and vulnerabilities, so do you. It's important you list all of them *specific to this opportunity*.

If you have clear advantages over other vendors, that's an important thing to consider when you are trying to decide whether to pursue a procurement or respond to an RFP. Likewise, if you have some serious disadvantages, some clear weaknesses that will hinder your ability to perform, that too is an important thing to consider.

It can sometimes be difficult to acknowledge when a competitor has advantages over you, but it's only by acknowledging your weaknesses that you can make good and responsible decisions about how to proceed.

> Understanding your competitive position is critical to making good bid/no bid decisions. All things considered, a good competitive position would clearly encourage responding to an RFP while a poor competitive position would discourage responding.

4. PRODUCTION CAPACITY

As a career salesperson, I admit I enthusiastically pursue almost every opportunity I find, and I'm not the only one. It's a trait built into our salesperson DNA; if we see something that might result in an opportunity, we start chasing it to see where it leads.

But somewhere in my professional development, I also learned that walking away from an opportunity is sometimes the most professional thing you can do. And one of the biggest reasons you should consider walking away is if you do not have the internal resources to deliver what the buyer is engaging you to provide.

Do you have the capacity to deliver the solution?

Depending on what you sell, answering this single question could result in hours and days of analysis and consideration. In general, though, there are three fundamental questions to ask:

- Do you have the equipment (or facilities or raw materials or whatever) you will need to deliver the work product?
- Do you have the professional talent to deliver the work product?
- Do you have the financial resources to fund the project or program while you're building or delivering it?

You have to decide whether you have the capacity based on the realities of your own business. Be honest with yourself. If you don't have the resources to deliver a project, don't bid on it.

> If your company does not have the resources to deliver the product or service the buyer is seeking, don't pursue it. They won't be happy with the product you deliver, it will hurt your reputation, and it probably won't be profitable.

5. PROPOSAL TEAM CAPACITY

I've worked with many companies over the years whose approach to RFPs was condensed into pithy phrases that each pledged fealty to the same "bid on everything" religion : "you can't win it if you don't bid it," "you have to bid it to win it," and "you can't win if you don't try."

In every one of these companies—every single one—the proposal team was worn out, burned out, and empty of all vitality. Moreover, their win rates were consistently low and their turnover rates were consistently high.

Does your proposal team have capacity to respond to another RFP?

Responding to formal procurements is not a numbers game; responding to more RFPs doesn't necessarily mean you're going to win more opportunities. In fact, it's often the opposite. If your proposal team is overworked, overburdened, and burnt out, the quality of the work they produce is likely going to decrease as proposal volume increases.

To be clear, in business development, it is sometimes necessary to work longer hours to complete a critical proposal. And for what it's worth, most of the proposal professionals I know embrace this reality; they are more than willing to step up to do their part to win a big deal for their company.

The problem is when "sometimes" turns into "all the time." If you consistently overburden your proposal team with too many RFPs, quality will surely suffer and your win rate will go down.

> **ⓘ** If your proposal team doesn't have capacity, don't try to jam another RFP into their workflow. It's not only counterproductive from a quality perspective, it will result in higher turnover in your proposal department.

6. PROFITABILITY

Why would anybody enter into any business relationship unless they thought they would make money rather than lose it? Despite this, there are some sales-driven companies that pursue almost every opportunity they find, even those that may not be profitable.

I've personally witnessed this many times. It usually occurs in cases where sales professionals are incented by commissions, not profits. Their mission is to make sales, so they pursue everything that might result in a sale. It's not their fault, really; they're just doing what they've been asked to do and what they are personally incented to do.

Will the program be profitable?

When deciding whether to bid or no-bid an RFP, responsible managers need to analyze the project or program to determine whether it will be profitable for their business. Every business and industry is different, so you have to decide what factors should be considered in your analysis.

Whatever factors you consider, though, just make sure you take the time to ask the question. Otherwise, you may end up winning new business that costs you more than it produces.

> **ⓘ** If a project or program is going to cost you more money than it makes, don't pursue it. Instead, find another opportunity that will return a profit for your business, and then invest your resources there.

PUTTING IT ALL TOGETHER

If you take everything we've just discussed and assemble it into a list, you have the beginnings of a checklist to guide your bid/no-bid decision process. Assemble your team, give everybody a copy of this list, or the custom list you created for your business, and start working through the topics.

1. Buyer familiarity
    1.1. Do you have a relationship?
    1.2. Do you know the decision makers?
    1.3. Do you know the influencers?
    1.4. Do they like you?
    1.5. Do you understand their history?
2. Requirements and capabilities
    2.1. Have you documented their requirements and do you have the capabilities to provide what they want?
    2.2. Do you have performance data?
3. Competitive assessment
    3.1. Do you know which vendors are competing?
    3.2. Does the RFP appear to favor a vendor?
    3.3. What are your competitors' strengths and weaknesses <u>specific to this opportunity</u>?
    3.4. What are your strengths and weaknesses <u>specific to this opportunity</u>?
4. Production capacity
    4.1. Do you have the capacity to deliver the solution?
5. Proposal team capacity
    5.1. Does your proposal team have the capacity to respond to another RFP?
6. Profitability
    6.1. Will the program be profitable?

Again, you have to create your own bid/no bid decision process that makes the most sense for your business, but hopefully this list will provide you with a good starting point.

HOW TO NO-BID

If you receive an RFP but decide to no-bid, it's important you share your decision with the buyer and tell them why. First, it's good business etiquette; it would be poor form not to. Second, it gives you the opportunity to tell the buyer you want to stay on the bidders list so you are included in future opportunities when they begin.

These letters should be simple and concise, and generally have four main parts.

1. Thank the person who sent you the RFP for inviting you to bid.

This is straightforward. Thank the person who invited you to bid, but make clear you are declining the invitation. Be sure to reference the bid number. Especially in busy procurement offices, this will help them to update their bidders list for the correct procurement.

2. Explain why you made the decision not to bid.

It's important to explain why you chose against bidding, but always state it in a way that puts your company in the best light. For example, DO NOT say, "We decided to no-bid because the RFP sounds like it was written to favor one of our competitors." Even if this is true, you'll accomplish little more than make the buyer angry. We all have enough hurdles in this world without adding more unnecessarily.

Usually, the best reasons to justify no-bidding are those that most business people will acknowledge without further explanation:

- We currently lack sufficient staff to support your project because all are assigned to other projects.
- We do not currently have the equipment or resources to implement your project on your timeline.
- The program you seek is a direction our company is heading, but we do not currently offer the functionality or systems called for in your RFP.
- The program you describe in your RFP requires XYZ, but currently, we only support the ZYX technology approach.

Hopefully, you're getting the idea. Provide some justification for why you are not bidding but keep it simple. Above all, keep it positive.

3. Explain you want to stay on their bidders list.

If you want to be considered for future projects or programs, say so. Otherwise, you may be removed from their list for future procurements.

4. Provide contact information

Provide contact information if they have immediate questions. A phone number and email address will usually suffice.

Example letter

Ultimately, notifying a buyer you do not intend to bid on their project should be simple, short, and to the point.

> *Dear John:*
>
> *Thank you for inviting us to bid on your RFP #12345 for IT development services. Unfortunately, we will not be submitting a bid.*
>
> *Though we have previously spoken with multiple people within your company, and were looking forward to working with you on a project like this one, our staff is currently fully engaged with multiple projects. Adding another project to the current workload would jeopardize work quality for everyone.*
>
> *Please know we remain interested in working with your firm, and we would like to remain on your list of bidders for future procurements.*
>
> *If you have any questions, please contact me at 123-456-7890, or at Jane@FictionalDevelopers.oops.*

11.

Scrutinizing the RFP

You thought this day would never come, but here it is. You finally got the RFP. Now what?

The first step in the process is to scrutinize the RFP. That is to say, you can't just read it, you have to analyze it. You have to evaluate it, ponder it, and consider it. Perhaps most important, you have to reconcile it against what you expected.

One of the best ways to scrutinize the RFP is by asking a series of questions. You make up your own list of questions, but here are some to begin with.

IS THE RFP WHAT YOU EXPECTED?

If you've been working with the buyer in the 12 to 24 months before the RFP is issued, you probably have a good understanding about what will be in the RFP based on what they told you they want. Now that the RFP is released and you scour its contents, ask yourself these two questions:

- Is there some requirement or specification you expected that was not included in the RFP?
- Is there some requirement or specification you did not expect that was included in the RFP?

Whenever you encounter RFP language you did not expect, it's usually worth your while to at least try and figure out what happened. Were you misinformed or did you misunderstand? Did something fundamental change at the last minute?

Just as important as knowing what happened is figuring out how it impacts what you're going to propose. Did the new language alter the solution you envisioned?

Always pay special attention to last minute changes because they can suggest internal events or decisions that aren't always apparent but that can impact or alter the buyer's direction.

ARE THERE ANY "SHOWSTOPPERS"?

This question is clear and straightforward: are there any showstoppers, any major requirements that you do not or cannot provide?

They're called "showstoppers" for a reason. When you're pursuing a sales opportunity but you encounter a showstopper, everything else should stop until you figure out if you can address the requirement, and if you can, whether you want to. If you cannot or do not want to, then walk away.

I'm making such a big deal about this because I periodically encounter enthusiastic salespeople who push forward on opportunities despite the presence of serious showstoppers. They do this because it's an RFP, an RFP represents an opportunity, and nobody in their right mind would ever walk away from an opportunity, right? Wrong. The reality is not every opportunity is a good opportunity, and sometimes, the most profitable customer is the one you walk away from.

WHAT ARE THE MAJOR REQUIREMENTS AND SPECIFICATIONS?

Most RFPs have a section where they list all of the major requirements every proposal must provide. *Use this list to make your list.*

In addition, as you scour the RFP, take time to identify sections of their proposal where they say things like "the provider will," "the provider shall," "the winning bidder must...," etc. These may not be listed discreetly in the requirements section, but they are requirements, nevertheless. Make sure you identify and document them now, so you'll be able to reference them in your proposal later.

HOW DO THEY EVALUATE / SCORE PROPOSALS?

Now, skip ahead to their decision criteria, to the section where they talk about how they are going to evaluate your proposal.

If your salespeople were successful during the pre-RFP selling phase of this effort, they've already identified how the buyer is going to "score" your proposal response. Read through the RFP version and reconcile the two.

If they align, great. If they don't, dig in further to understand why they don't align. Did you miss something before or did they change their evaluation approach? It's important to understand why.

IS THERE ANY LANGUAGE FAVORING A COMPETITOR?

Do you see any questions or requirements that seem to either favor a particular vendor or disqualify a group of vendors?

- **Favor a particular vendor.** You have to know your competition well if you're going to be effective at picking these out. You have to be able to look at a question and say, "this was taken from ABC Company's sales brochure." The good news is when buyers use this approach, they're often rather clumsy. They tend to recite the other vendor's talking points or sales message just a little bit too accurately. This makes them easy to pick out.
- **Disqualifying a group of vendors.** Sometimes, buyers that favor a particular vendor don't write their RFPs to favor one vendor as much as to disqualify the other vendors who are not their favorite. If they mandate a red office copier, and only one company sells a red copier while the rest of the industry only sells blue office copiers, they are effectively disqualifying everyone except for the vendor they want.

When you encounter this kind of language, you can save yourself a lot of time and effort by recognizing the procurement has been preordained for someone else to win. No matter what you propose or how great your price, you've already lost and your competitor has already won.

WHAT HAS CHANGED FROM THEIR LAST RFP TO THIS ONE?

Do you save and catalogue all of the RFPs you receive? If you answer yes, kudos to you. You deserve a gold medal, an attaboy, and yes, maybe even a pay raise. If you answer no, you should start. This is _**huge**_ (and please notice _**huge**_ is bold, italic, _and_ underlined because yes, it's that huge).

When you get an RFP today, one of the top issues on your mind, or that should be on your mind, is knowing what's most important to the buyer _today_. There are many ways to learn this, a relationship with the decision maker being the best. But another great way is to compare and contrast today's RFP with the last one the buyer published for the same contract.

> Figure out what's different between their last RFP and the current RFP and you've found something that's important today that wasn't before.

Suppose the previous RFP talks about customer service response times once in the entire document. This RFP, in contrast, addresses customer service response times in five places over ten pages. Not only that, they get detailed; they ask probing questions, ask for process definitions, and require service level agreements built around response times. When you see something like this, something important has changed from the last RFP to this one. It's important because, in all likelihood, it's a pain point.

- Is the current vendor falling short or have they totally failed?
- Is there a new program manager in place who wants to emphasize vendor responsiveness?

Whatever it is, something has clearly changed and your job is to figure out what that something is. Even if you don't, though, you've still learned something valuable as you prepare to respond to this RFP; since it wasn't important before, but it is obviously important now, you had better find a way to address it prominently in your proposal.

Save past RFPs and refer to them. You'll be glad you did.

ARE THERE ANY ITEMS THAT ARE NOT CLEAR?

Be sure to write down any items that are not clear or that could be interpreted multiple ways. Then submit those questions to the buyer—something most RFPs allow.

One of the worst things that can happen is when you get to the writing portion of your project—after vendor questions have been submitted and responded to—and you realize you still have substantive questions.

12.

Proposal Kickoff Meeting Part 1: Compiling and Analyzing What You've Learned

Most proposal kickoff meetings are too administrative. They're more focused on project management functions—like assigning RFP questions and establishing deadlines—than defining a strategy to win the sale.

This does not negate or even minimize the importance of project management. Every proposal development project should have a senior manager who has the ability to hand out assignments and establish deadlines, and the authority to bring down Thor's Hammer on anyone who neglects their assigned responsibilities. It's a critical part of the overall project.

Still, at its most fundamental, an RFP is not a writing project to complete, it's a sales opportunity to win.

An RFP is not a writing project to complete, it's a sales opportunity to win.

This means proposal kickoff meetings should be primarily about sales strategy, about figuring out the solution you need to offer and how you need to message it.

Correctly structured, an effective proposal kickoff meeting has three main parts, each of which we are going to discuss over this and the next two chapters.

- **Part 1**: Compiling and making sense of what you've learned
- **Part 2**: Configuring your solution
- **Part 3**: Configuring your message

Only after you accomplish these three tasks do you begin assigning RFP questions and deadlines to your staff.

COMPILING AND SHARING WHAT YOU KNOW

In an ideal world, everyone on your business development team has been involved in the opportunity as it progressed through the pre-RFP selling process, and they've been receiving regular progress reports on what's been learned. In real life, this doesn't always happen.

Therefore, the first part of your proposal kickoff meeting is to assemble your team—salespeople, proposal writers and manager, subject matter experts, relevant operations staff, senior managers—and brief everyone about everything you've learned.

Structure your briefing

The briefing you prepare for your team should loosely follow both the information you collected during the pre-RFP selling phase and the insights you gained while doing a deep dive analysis of the RFP. Use the following outline as a place to start, but don't be ruled by it. Adjust it to suit your needs.

1. **Describe the program**.
   1.1. Describe the project or program.
   1.2. Explain what the buyer wants in the new program, and describe how the contract has changed over time.

1.3. Describe any grievances they have, successes they've experienced, challenges they've faced, and any opportunities you can leverage in your solution.

2. **Discuss the current vendor.**

   2.1. Provide a detailed accounting of the current vendor including how well they're doing in the eyes of the decision makers.

   2.2. Identify instances where they're falling short.

   2.3. Identify instances where they're unusually strong.

   2.4. Identify opportunities where they are weak and you are strong.

   2.5. Include an accounting of the vendors who have handled the program over the years.

3. **Identify the individual decision makers and the non-decision-making influencers, including the following...**

   3.1. Their titles and roles.

   3.2. Their influence within the decision-making process.

   3.3. Their personal vendor preferences.

   3.4. Their personal motivations and objectives.

   3.5. Their personal perceptions of risk.

   3.6. Whether they are champions, antagonists, or non-committal.

   3.7. Describe any other information you discover for each decision maker or influencer that you might be able to use, highlight, or make subtle references to in your proposal.

4. **Explain the circumstances.**

   4.1. Explain why they are issuing the RFP now.

   4.2. Document any relevant circumstances (a change in management, the current vendor is failing, etc.).

5. **Share their decision criteria and selection process.**

   5.1. Identify the model or process they are using to choose a vendor or product.

   5.2. Document the criteria they will be using to make a purchase decision.

   5.3. Explain their point scoring system/award process and your evaluation of it.

6. **Share observations from your earlier RFP assessment.**

6.1. Describe any RFP content you did not expect.

6.2. Identify any "showstoppers" you discovered.

6.3. List the major requirements and specs they list in their RFP, and whether there was anything that diverged from your expectations.

6.4. Identify any language that favors or appears to favor a competitor.

6.5. Present any RFP language that changed from their last RFP to this one.

6.6. Identify any RFP language or requirements that are not clear and need to be clarified.

7. **Share anything else that is relevant.**

This outline is a good place to begin, but it isn't written in stone. You should take the time to create your own template that works best for you and your team.

However you choose to organize it, it's critical your briefing is sufficiently comprehensive so your business development team is fully informed. Only then will they be able to participate meaningfully in the sales strategy aspects of your kickoff meeting that follow.

How to share your briefing

You may choose to deliver this briefing in person. Depending on the makeup of your group, this might make sense.

Like most business people, though, I prefer meetings to be as streamlined as possible. To that end, you may consider drafting a briefing document and then sharing it with participants ahead of the kickoff meeting. This gives them a chance to review the briefing at their own pace, and it shortens meeting length. Obviously, it is important to stress that participants have to make the time to actually read and consider the briefing document you prepare. This approach doesn't work if people don't read it.

Then, when you convene the meeting, begin by reviewing some of the high points of the briefing document and invite questions. These meetings are most beneficial when participants are engaged and feel comfortable asking questions and participating in discussions.

PROCESSING INFORMATION INTO INTELLIGENCE

So far, you've spent 12-24 months collecting information, and you just shared all of the relevant information with your team. Now it's time to turn that information into actionable intelligence.

Process and outcome

The way I prefer to transform raw information into intelligence is to ask a series of questions.

Process: asking questions

In modern Western culture, we routinely use the term *dialogue* interchangeably with words like conversation, a discussion between two or more people. In our kickoff meeting, though, I want to use it more like Socrates and Plato did, as a didactic or learning device built around conversational exchange. In other words, *thinking out loud together*.

The way this works, I offer a comment or observation about something. You hear what I'm saying and respond, "Yea, I see where you're going with this. What if we did this...?" Then someone else chimes in, "Yes, we're redefining the problem. I like this. How about we say it this way...?" And then we're off, working cooperatively, throwing out ideas, considering different perspectives, etc. See the point? We're working together as a team to use our collective creativity to build a better result; *we're thinking out loud together*.

This chapter includes a list of questions intended to inspire this dialogue.

Outcome: actionable intelligence

Buyers do not want stock answers copied and pasted from other RFPs. They want custom solutions, configured expressly for them, that address the things that concern them the most. To that end, the outcome you hope to achieve from this questioning process is to distill everything you've collected into actionable intelligence. This intelligence will guide both how you build your customer-focused solution and how you formulate your messaging in your proposal.

Questions to ask and answer

Consider the following list of questions as a prototype, a starting point. Then customize the list to make it your own so it best reflects your business and your team's needs.

1. What is their primary issue, problem, or objective?

Over the course of my selling career, I've come to learn there are many things buyers care about, but there is almost always just one thing that matters more than all the others. This is their primary issue, this is what's driving their decision, and this is where you need to focus your attention and effort.

If a university is building a new stadium complex, for example, they may have a number of important issues they care about, but the most important is finishing the project on time. They need it completed by a specific date because they have some future events scheduled that require the new structure's capacity.

Since this requirement is so important, it's critical to share it with your business development team, and emphasize how important it is to the buyer's decision making.

2. What are their next five major issues and requirements?

An RFP may include a hundred different requirements to which you must comply, so you may be wondering why I am focusing so much time and attention on just the top five or six. Good question.

Compliance is a thing. If they list a requirement, you have to indicate whether or not you comply. All of the requirements are important or they wouldn't be requirements. But often, most of the requirements are more like 'checkmark' items.

A checkmark item is where the customer asks if you have it. If you answer in the affirmative, they say, "OK, check that one off the list. What's the next question." In other words, these are items that could disqualify you if you don't have them, but they aren't going to win you the deal.

> RFP requirement: All work trucks must have four tires.
>
> Reviewer: Do their trucks have four tires? Yes. OK, check that one off the list. Next question?

> RFP requirement: All external doors must have locks.
>
> Reviewer: Are they putting locks on all the external doors? Yes. OK, check that one off the list. Next question?

The point is this: sellers need to be compliant with the buyer's requirements, but they should focus most of their attention on the requirements the buyer cares about most, the ones that will actually win them the business.

Therefore, after agreeing on the buyer's primary issue, your next task is to agree on the next five major issues that concern the buyer. Be sure to prioritize your list based on how important each item is to the buyer.

Building on the previous construction example, you and your team identified five major requirements that will influence the outcome of the procurement:

1. Incorporating a large, multi-level parking garage because they're currently landlocked and short on space.
2. Completing the project without impacting ongoing campus operations.
3. Ensuring an airtight site security plan because adventurous college students can sometimes get curious and wander onto job sites.
4. Demonstrating to the local community the project is being completed with local labor and contractors.
5. Incorporating environmentally friendly building practices so the resulting structure is as "green" as possible.

Every RFP includes a long list of requirements, but how well you address these top five issues determines whether you win their business.

3. What are the personal motivations driving these requirements?

In previous chapters, we discussed how it's important to understand the buyer's requirements, but we also discussed the importance of understanding the personal motivations that resulted in the requirements.

In the previous example, they list a site security plan as a requirement. This is nothing unusual, but the backstory adds dimension to the requirement. A group of inebriated students wandered onto the site of their last building project and one was injured. It looked bad for the school, they were sued in court, and though the student recovered and the suit was settled, it gave them a black eye. They don't want anything like that to ever happen again.

Knowing the backstory helps your writers to more effectively address the true motivations behind the requirement.

4. What differentiates you from other vendors?

When choosing a vendor for a strategically important project, many buyers begin by disqualifying vendors until they're left with a couple or a few who are each well qualified to perform the work. Then they ask the all-important question: "Of these three vendors, which is best for us?"

The most successful salespeople don't leave it to buyers to answer that question on their own, they help the buyer by proactively showcasing and highlighting the ways their solution is both different and better than what anyone else is offering.

At this point in the kickoff meeting, your entire business development team needs to come together to identify the most relevant and compelling things that differentiate your solution from competitive alternatives. This usually involves lots of discussion and sometimes even spirited debate. Just remember the best differentiators do three things well.

- **Opportunity specific.** Effective differentiators are opportunity specific, not market general. Instead of saying you have the largest warehouse on the East coast, explain how you already stock 100 of the items they order most frequently in sufficient quantity for their needs.

- **Aligned with buyer needs**. Effective differentiators must be aligned with buyer needs. Don't cite awards you've won from small business associations if you're selling to a multinational conglomerate.

- **Different and better**. It's not enough to be different. Effective differentiators must show how your solution is both different and better than what anyone else is offering.

As you identify your differentiators, add them to a list. You'll figure out how to express them later.

Identifying differentiators is arduous work, but it's one of the more critical things you'll do. Invest enough time in this effort to do it well.

5. What does the buyer perceive are their greatest risks?

We talked previously about the importance of understanding the individual motivations of the decision makers and influencers you meet. People are motivated by many different things, of course, but one of the most universally powerful motivators of all is the perception of risk.

Risk is a personal perception, but that doesn't make it any less real to the person feeling it. This is why it is critical for sellers to identify perceptions of risk; if not addressed, risk can kill a sale faster than just about anything else.

Suppose a government agency is looking for a vendor to manage a program. The last vendor they hired looked great on paper, but they had financial difficulties and went out of business before the contract was completed. As a consequence, the senior decision makers involved in the procurement share a perception of risk; they can't allow the same thing to happen again. If you want a shot at winning their business, therefore, you have to both address the risk and prove you have the financial and organizational staying power to complete the contract term.

Understanding their perception of risk is critical to addressing their concerns and winning their business.

6. What are your greatest competitive risks and weaknesses?

Just as important as identifying the things that differentiate your solution, that give you an advantage, you must also identify the competitive risks you face and the weakness you have to overcome.

If one of your competitors has a strong support organization in the buyer's region, and your support organization is comparatively meager, you cannot ignore it. You have to both acknowledge it and then figure out how you're going to deal with it.

Take the time and make the effort to identify your competitive risks, your weaknesses, and address them.

ACTIONABLE INTELLIGENCE IS YOUR OBJECTIVE

In the next two chapters, you are going to configure the solution you are going to propose and the messaging you are going to use to communicate it. But you can't do any of those things unless you've first taken the time to distill everything you've learned into actionable intelligence.

13.

Proposal Kickoff Meeting Part 2: Configuring Your Solution

A product is a product. A service is a service. A solution is something we build for a client who is trying to solve a problem. The solution may include one or more of our products or services, but they are each—product, service, and solution—unique things.

Suppose you sell office copiers. You've got big copiers, small copiers, red copiers, blue copiers, standalone copiers, networked copiers—all kinds of copiers. These copiers are not your solution, per se, they are the machines that make up your product line. OK so far?

You may sell the exact same copier to three unique businesses, but you are not selling the same solution to each buyer. In the three fictional examples that follow, each customer is unique, and each requires a unique solution custom built for their needs.

- Sally at Mom's Corner Store needs a small, inexpensive copier that she can use to receive faxes from her vendors and make copies of invoices before she mails them out to her credit customers. She needs an installment payment plan because she doesn't have lots of cash flow. She also needs someone who can set up the machine because, while she's great at running a general store, she doesn't know a thing about electronics.

- Jack at the local library needs the same copier as Sally, but he needs a coin device attached to it so people can pay to make copies. He's pretty good with the maintenance part of it; he can set it up himself and replenish the paper and toner, but because it's a revenue source for the library, he needs prompt service if the copier ever breaks.
- Suzy runs a small mortgage closing agency and is required, by law, to provide each client with a copy of each document at the closing, before they leave her office. She doesn't have a huge volume of business—she is semi-retired, after all—but whatever she buys, she wants to be confident that her copier will be working when she needs it so she'll never have to reschedule a closing.

These are simple examples, but they illustrate the point well. You are selling the exact same copier to each buyer, but if you're doing your job well, you are packaging that copier in a solution *wrapper* that is built custom for each buyer.

- For Sally, you include a 12 months same as cash program so she can afford it, you agree to deliver it and set it up for her, and you agree to stop by and replace her toner cartridge when it gets low.
- For Jack, you attach a coin-operated device so people at the library can pay to make copies. You also include your one-hour response service plan so if the copier ever stops working, someone is there to fix it within the hour. One final thing—and the one thing Jack appreciates more than the rest—you offer to pass out flyers around town to help get out the word about the library's new pay-to-make-copies service.
- For Suzy, you're providing the same copier you did for Sally and Jack, but you propose two copiers instead of just one. This redundancy means she will never have to reschedule a mortgage closing because her copier isn't working.

See the point? You're selling the same copier to each customer, but because they each have unique requirements, you've created a unique solution for each one.

WHY IS ALL THIS IMPORTANT IN AN RFP/PROPOSAL CONTEXT?

When an organization gets an RFP, too many sellers are too quick to sit down and start typing answers to questions. In other words, they're treating the RFP like it's a questionnaire, a fill-in-the-blank form used to capture product features and capabilities. What they ARE NOT doing is taking time to figure out what they're selling—the actual solution they're going to propose—before they dive in. They are relinquishing their professional sales role to devolve into product peddlers and features preachers.

I was explaining this concept to one client and he pushed back: "We sell data support services. It doesn't matter who we're selling to, we sell the same basic service." Whenever someone says something like this, my initial reaction is that he hasn't dug deep enough to find out more about the customer, their needs and concerns, and how he can appeal to what's important to them. So that's what we did, we dug deeper.

Before long, our effort produced results. We learned the manager who leads my customer's technical support group was well known to the buyer; he had actually worked for the buyer in an earlier job. Further, the buyer thinks highly of him and his abilities. Once we learned this tidbit, we made the support manager an integral part of the solution we were proposing. He was skilled and able, talented at solving problems remotely, and because he had worked there, he was already familiar with the buyer's firm. This manager's involvement ultimately turned out to be a large and compelling component of the solution we were proposing.

The point is you can't just sell the same product or service to every client and call it a solution. You actually have to take time to configure a unique solution for each unique client—and you need to do this before you start working on messaging. This is precisely what this portion of your kickoff meeting is focused on doing.

1. Configure and summarize the solution

This is where your business development team creates and drafts the solution you want to propose. Your solution should mention all of the relevant components the customer will want to know.

Please note we are not yet discussing messaging, that comes later. All we're doing now is using the intelligence we collected in the previous step to build the solution that will best address what the buyer says they want. Here's how we might structure a solution for Suzy at Suzy's Mortgage Closing Service.

- *The solution we are proposing to Suzy's Mortgage Closing Service includes two OfficeMaster5000 copiers. Having two identical copiers ensures she never has to postpone a mortgage closing because a copier isn't working.*

- *Sam will be doing the installation. Sam has done copier service work for Suzy before and she respects his ability. They like each other and get along well.*

- *Though we are proposing two copiers, we are saving her money by charging for the basic service plan, not the premium plan. Since our solution includes a backup copier, it's not imperative for her to have the premium plan's one-hour service if one of the copiers breaks. This, alone, makes our solution closer in price to the single copier plus one-hour service option she had previously been considering.*

- *We're giving her a 7% manufacturer's discount because she's buying two machines. This, and the savings from the basic service plan, puts our solution in the same ball park with the competition—despite the redundancy of having two copiers—which she likes.*

- *We're promising delivery within a week of signing the contract. Our competitor is quoting her a three-week delivery on their machine.*

This is obviously a fictional and simple example, but it illustrates the point. It's important everyone in your kickoff meeting understands the totality of the solution you're proposing and the story behind it. With this knowledge and background, when they sit down to write their assigned sections, they'll be able to draft content that is more customer-focused.

2. Include non-traditional components that add value

When you think like a seller, you often think in terms of what you're selling. When you think like a buyer, though, you tend to view what they are buying in a more comprehensive, holistic way—not just what they're buying but the totality of what they get.

> It's not about what you're selling, it's about the totality of what they get.

Sometimes, oftentimes, the things buyers value most have nothing to do with the product or service you're selling but the little things that make their lives easier. Here are a few examples.

Notification of legislative or regulatory updates

One of my clients operated in an industry that was heavily regulated by the federal government and separately by each state government. Because they were a national organization, they tracked and compiled all of the regulations and court decisions both at the federal and the state level. What's great is they shared this with their clients.

Their clients did not pay for this information, they paid for a separate, related service and this was just an add-on. But this information proved valuable to the buyers who received it. They were able to use it and benefit from it, even though they didn't actually pay for it.

It's not what you're selling, it's what they get.

An invoicing department that's easy to work with

One client I worked with had a client base made up entirely of small organizations with relatively limited internal resources. After interviewing some of these small-organization clients, we learned that one of the things they liked most about us was how easy we were to work with. And this sentiment was most pronounced in our invoicing practices.

In this particular industry, there are many line items that make up an invoice. My client had a sophisticated system to track each line item, and then to present them to their client in a way that was easy to understand. The seller also had a great service in place where their clients could call Janice in accounting to ask about individual items. Janice was easy going, likeable, and more important, she was a wiz at quickly figuring out whatever question or issue the buyer raised. This made it easy on the buyer's limited-resource accounting department—something the buyers very much appreciated. It was entirely incidental to my client's primary offering, but it was huge to their customers.

It's not what you're selling, it's what they get.

14.

Proposal Kickoff Meeting Part 3: Configuring Your Sales Message

So far, you've spent considerable time in your kickoff meeting understanding the circumstances surrounding the bid, discussing the buyer and their needs, and configuring the solution you want to propose. As you transition into this next phase of the meeting, your goal is to decide how you want to communicate your solution to the buyer.

To be clear, the solution you create is different from the messaging you use to communicate it. The *solution* solves their problem, but the *messaging* is how you explain it to them. It's the way you tell them how your solution is going to get them what they want.

PROCESS AND OUTCOME

The process you use during this phase of your meeting is to ask a series of questions. The outcome you hope to achieve from this process is to create a list of talking points that all of your staff can refer to when drafting content.

Process: asking questions

Earlier in our kickoff meeting, we used this technique to consider all of the information we had collected and then transform it into actionable intelligence. We're going to use the same technique here—ask and answer a series of questions—but this time, we're going to use it to configure out sales message.

Outcome: talking points

One of the best ways to configure your sales message for this kind of project is to create a series of talking points. This is just like the talking points you always hear about on political news shows. You are boiling down your story, your message, into a list of concise sentences or phrases that are easy to recall and then articulate.

Then, everyone who leaves the meeting will have a list of the exact same talking points. They may express them differently depending on the context, but everyone is still communicating the exact same message.

Using an example opportunity to explain

In my experience teaching this section in training classes—trying to illustrate both the process and the talking points to produce—I've found it's much easier if we have an example opportunity to pursue. So before slogging ahead, let's pause a moment and draft an example opportunity we can use to explore this approach.

Example opportunity: Donna's Fictional Coffee Cups wants a payroll solution

We are Dave's Fictional Payroll Processing Company and we are trying to make a sale to Donna's Fictional Coffee Cups. Earlier in our kickoff meeting, we identified Donna's primary reason for issuing the RFP; they're expanding and they need a payroll company that can keep up.

> *Donna's has been expanding both in size and geography. The payroll processing vendor they've been using is a small, local shop, and not well equipped to handle their expansion. They're looking for a new payroll processing vendor that is large enough to handle their needs as they grow but is still able to provide local support in each of the cities where they operate.*

Because we understand Donna's objectives so well, we configured a solution to ensure they get what they want. We defined it this way.

> *We are assigning Bob, one of our senior veteran operations staff, to be the primary account manager to Donna's central office. Bob already has a working relationship with the controller there, Sally. They know each other through a number of shared associations, and they previously worked at the same accounting department in the same company.*
>
> *The RFP says they have seven offices in as many cities. In the solution we configured, we are proposing that each of our office managers in each of those cities is assigned to each senior manager in each of their offices. Further, each of these office managers becomes a part of the account team under Bob's leadership. Their senior managers were not listed in the RFP, but we identified them previously and reached out to each of them over the last six months to introduce ourselves, so they know who we are.*

City	Our account staff	Their senior manager at that office
Cincinnati	Bob Jones	Sally Smith
Columbus	Joe Johnson	Barb Bartinelli
Cleveland	Lisa Lo	Chris Crane
Indianapolis	Paul Puff	Doug Double
Lexington	Carol Comber	Suzy Sierra
Louisville	Jamie Jesse	Tracey Tongo
Chicago	Becky Beaufort	Chris Calico

> *This arrangement will satisfy their primary requirements: we're large enough to serve all of their offices as they expand, but we also have a local account team in place to provide personalized service to each office.*

Now that we've defined our example opportunity, including the problem they're experiencing and the solution we've configured to address it, we can advance to the subject of this chapter—*messaging*. Specifically, we need to figure out how to create and communicate a sales message the buyer finds compelling.

QUESTIONS TO ASK AND ANSWER

In part one of your kickoff meeting, you asked a series of questions to turn the information you had collected into actionable intelligence. Then you used the intelligence to guide how you formulated the solution.

You're going to continue the same process here. This involves using the intelligence you created to help you build targeted messaging. Remember, your purpose for asking questions is not to get quick answers but to inspire dialogue. You want to encourage each member of your business development team, including each person helping to develop content, to participate and contribute to the discussion.

1. How is the solution you are proposing going to address the buyer's primary issue?

In answering this first question, in building your talking points, you need to fill out a table with three columns:
- The customer's issue
- Your solution
- The benefit the buyer receives

It's important to summarize your comments into concise snippets. You can get really detailed, if you want, but I advise against it. Everyone who is going to be using these talking points to draft content has been participating in the meeting so you don't have to recap every detail. Fewer points, clearly stated, make it easier for your writers to draft compelling, customer-focused content.

The customer's issue	Our approach	The benefit the customer receives
They want coverage today	We mapped each of our offices to each of their offices in each city. We have the geographic coverage to serve their entire organization today.	*No delay or ramp up. We have the infrastructure, in place today, to serve their needs.*
Coverage as they expand	We identified the cities they are planning to expand into over the next 36 months. We confirmed we now have, or will have, offices in each of those cities.	*No uncertainty or unpredictability; we have or will have the infrastructure to serve their future offices as they come online.*
Local support for each office	We built an account team, headed by Bob, that provides for each local office manager to work individually with each of their office managers at each of their locations. That equals local support.	*You aren't losing anything by switching to a larger firm. Even though we are larger than your current vendor, we have the local support to provide personal service to each office across your enterprise.*

This simple table fully encapsulates the messaging you want to communicate whenever you're discussing their primary issue.

2. Focus on the other buying requirements: how is the solution you are proposing going to address/solve the next five issues?

Just like you created talking points for their main issue, you must also create talking points for each of the secondary issues they care about. You need to start by acknowledging the buyer's issue, then summarize your solution, and then articulate what they get by choosing your solution.

Getting back to the payroll example

In an earlier segment of the sales proposal meeting, you identified the five secondary issues that the buyer, Donna's Fictional Coffee Cups, is seeking from any solution you build for them:

- The vendor must offer checks, pay cards, and direct deposit.
- The vendor must be able to accept and process payroll files submitted in a broad array of file types from timekeeping systems to Excel spreadsheets to flat files.
- The buyer's staff must have easy access to managers who have both the knowledge and authority to fix problems quickly.
- Especially for some of their smaller, remote offices, the vendor must provide patient, helpful service—hand holding—so their less-experienced staff can set up new employees with minimal effort or frustration.
- The vendor must provide their staff with quarterly briefings on changes to regulations or tax laws that impact their business or employees.

With these issues documented, your task here is to create talking points for each of the secondary issues that are important to the buyer.

Their issue	Our approach	The benefit the customer receives
Each employee should be able to choose how they are paid.	Each employee can choose their own method of compensation: a paper check, a debit card, or an electronic deposit directly into their account.	*Not all of your employees have checking accounts, and it costs them to go somewhere to cash their paychecks. With payment cards, they can now have access to their full pay without penalty.*
Across their organization, their offices submit payroll in three different file types.	We can accept payroll files in a wide variety of formats, from electronic transfer to manual submission.	*Until you consolidate to a single format, which is what you said you want to do, none of your offices has to change how they submit payroll records. We accept all you currently use, and we have systems in place to ensure each transmission is received accurately. This minimizes the time you have to invest in reconciliation and recovery.*
Access to authority to fix problems.	Your program manager has a direct line to our senior operations manager.	*If you ever encounter a problem, and you aren't satisfied with how we solved it at your local office, you can call Jane, our VP of Operations. Jane has the authority, expertise, and motivation to fix it and make you happy.*

"Hand holding" level of service for remote offices.	We have included our senior office managers, in each city where your offices are located, as part of our account team.	*Each of our managers in each of the cities where you operate will contact your staff to build a one-to-one working relationship. If there is ever an issue, our local office manager will personally walk them through to resolution.*
Regular regulatory updates.	We monitor legislative and regulatory changes. As a client, we share our findings with you.	*You will always be aware of the most recent changes to laws or regulations that impact your operations. This helps you stay compliant without costing you anything additional.*

3. How are your competitive advantages going to benefit the buyer?

In a previous chapter, *Proposal Kickoff Meeting Part 1*, you identified a list of differentiators, the things that make your solution both different and better than competing alternatives. At this point in the kickoff meeting, your goal is to figure out how to express those differentiators so they are buyer-focused.

Differentiator	Explanation	The message...
They love our account manager, Bob	They've been working with Bob for many years. They know him and they trust him. They want to keep working with him.	*Bob is our employee. If they work with us, they get to work with Bob. None of our competitors have Bob.*

Geographic proximity	We have an office within 10 miles of each of their offices. We also have offices in the three cities they're thinking of expanding into.	*Unlike some other payroll processing firms that lack local presence, our close proximity means we can be more responsive to their needs; if they have an issue, we can be onsite within an hour.*
New invoicing system streamlines invoicing and payment	We have a new, state of the art accounting and invoicing system that streamlines the entire invoicing and payment process. This is one of the things they've been complaining about with their current vendor. Their vendor's system is error-prone, and if they have questions, it's difficult for them to find answers.	*Unlike their current vendor, our new system will improve accuracy and minimize their administrative overhead reconciling invoicing issues.*

When your staff walks out of this meeting and back to their cubicles, these talking points make certain they clearly understand the things that make you different and better than the competition.

4. How are you going to explain why your competitors' advantages are irrelevant?

As we work our way through our messaging discussion, you need to spend at least some time talking about your competitors, the advantages they have or may claim to have over you, and how you are going to undermine or minimize their claims.

Many sellers don't like this exercise. When you're focusing on their advantages over you, it feels defeatist. Still, it's a powerful and effective exercise if you're willing to make the effort and learn from it. It will allow you to more intelligently position your solutions against your competitors' solutions.

Build a table that has three columns:

- The competitors' advantages
- An explanation
- How you are going to address it

The Competitors' Advantages	Explanation	How we address it
They offer a lower price	XYZ Payroll company offers a lower price for their basic service, but they nickel and dime for every additional service you want.	*It's important to compare apples to apples. Our price may appear higher than some of our competitors, but we charge one flat fee for our service. Unlike some others, we never charge for extra file types or payment methods. With our service, you can budget more accurately and predictably.*
They are significantly larger than we are	Their company is huge. They have lots of cash, lots of resources, lots of people, and they have name brand recognition in the larger market.	*While some of our competitors may be larger, don't get confused because that's not comparing apples to apples. Their payroll processing group, which is one small division of their overall enterprise, is about the same size as our company. In other words, they aren't any larger than we are, but unlike them, our entire business is focused on payroll services for companies like yours.*

If you are going to tell the buyer how your solution is different and better, you should expect your competitor will do the same. If you can ghost the competition, though, if you can show the weaknesses of their arguments and provide information that will prompt the buyer to ask more questions of your competition, you will advance your cause.

5. How are you going to explain your shortcomings?

As a proposal consultant with years of experience working for many sellers, I can tell you with certainty that I have never seen a perfect solution. Every solution has a shortcoming or a blemish or an ugly wart. Some are even plagued with afflictions so severe they're deal breakers.

Do not avoid them, confront them.

As a team, you need to identify these shortcomings, you need to agree how serious they are, and then you need to figure out how you're going to address them. The following table is one way to organize this information.

Shortcoming	Seriousness	How we address it
They have expressed interest in expanding into Canada at some point in the future. They want a vendor that can support them there.	**Not too serious.** Their conversations about this have so far been casual, but no real plans and no real determination. Advise we don't even address it unless we have to.	*If it does come up..."Like you, we have also considered expanding our business into Canada. Though we aren't there now, we have done considerable research already, and we could implement an expansion with relatively little delay."*
They require we have an independent audit to confirm we have security measures in place	**Serious.** We have security measures, and we just hired a Security Officer to bolster our security program, but have	*1. Admit we don't have external certification today. 2. Explain what we have done (robust security infrastructure, hiring a new security officer, etc.).*

to protect their employees' data.	not yet engaged an outside organization to perform an audit.	*3. Promise to engage an external security audit within three months of being awarded the contract. 4. Emphasize we have never had a security breach in our ten years in business.*

If it's a relatively insignificant shortcoming, maybe you choose to not say anything. If it's a major shortcoming, though, not saying anything is like trying to host a cocktail party with a great, big elephant standing in the middle of the room. It's useless to ignore the elephant, especially when everyone sees him (and probably smells him, too). You have to figure out how to address it. If it's a really huge shortcoming, maybe you choose not to respond.

Just make sure everyone on your team understands the shortcomings and how you're going to address them before they go off to write their proposal content sections.

6. How are you going to defuse the buyer's perceptions of risk?

In an earlier part of our meeting, we identified perceptions of risk within the buyer's organization. Now, in the messaging portion of the meeting, we have to figure out how we're going to address those perceptions.

Identified Risk	Source	How we address it
Concern about the size and stability of the company they hire. The last two firms they hired went out	A generalized concern across the organization, though the loudest voice is Sally in accounting. She's	*We need to stress that we are a stable organization. 1. We are profitable, and have been every year since we launched. 2. We are growing, but we regulate our growth so we don't suffer cash flow problems. 3. We have a $5M*

of business before the contract was complete.	the one who's had to fix everything after the other two firms went out of business.	*line of credit, but we have no debt. We are a stable and ongoing concern.*

7. What is your style and tone?

Have you ever read a proposal that appears as though it was written by ten different people? It probably was, but it shouldn't sound that way. It should sound like it was written by a single person using a consistent style and tone. Clearly, it's difficult to make a single document with multiple authors sound like it was written by one, but there are a few things you can do to improve your chances.

Use present tense most of the time

The popular style manuals handle this question differently. For proposal writing, though, I recommend using present tense most of the time because it sounds more decisive, more certain. Consider these examples.

- **Future tense**: The payroll program we are proposing will provide a better way to reconcile your payroll files with actual payables.
- **Present tense**: The payroll program we are proposing provides a better way to reconcile your payroll files with actual payables.

I know, I know, it's a small detail. And admittedly, you aren't going to win a deal just by switching all of your writing to present tense from future tense. Still, writing in present tense sounds stronger and, as I said, more certain. It's the difference between, "we do this already," and "if you hire us, we promise to do this."

Whatever you decide, make sure everyone uses the same tense.

Use active voice

On a LinkedIn discussion board many years back, there was a conversation about active voice vs. passive voice. One discussion participant, Frank Karlin, illustrated well what it sounds like when you're using the passive. I'm paraphrasing, but he suggested the next time you leave for work in the morning, try saying something like this:

> *You are loved, and will be seen tonight.*

I laughed out loud when I read this, and I can almost hear the startled response: "Wait! I am loved? By whom? And who's going to see me tonight? Come back here and explain yourself!"

We've all been taught to write in active voice, and this humorous example clarifies why. Passively written sentences are squirrely and unclear. They're ambiguous. In fact, they're only useful when your goal is to not say something clearly.

Active voice, in contrast, has two advantages: clarity and credibility.

Active voice advantage #1: clarity

Sentences written in the active voice are clear. Their construction is straight forward, not ambiguous, and generally easier to understand. They say things like, "I love you," not, "you are loved." With the active voice, you know it's me who loves you. With the passive, you're just guessing who's doing the loving.

Active voice advantage #2: credibility

People who write in active voice sound more credible. And because they SOUND more credible, they ARE more credible—if only in the mind of the reader.

This idea of credibility is so important because your perceived credibility and the buyer's perception of risk are inextricably linked. Proposals exist within the context of a sales transaction, and there is almost always some perception of risk in a sales transaction. You're trying to convince someone to choose your product or service that they will use in some strategic or mission critical function. This in itself is risky. You're also trying to convince them to part with their money. Both of these things contribute to a buyer's perception of risk.

No one will adopt your solution or part with their money if they do not perceive you as credible. The less credibility you have, the greater sense of risk they have, and the less likely you are to make a sale. Conversely, the more credible you are, the less risk they perceive, and the more likely you are to make a sale.

Active voice will not, by itself, make you credible or your writing clear. But writing in the active voice will contribute to your efforts to write clearly and establish yourself and your company as being credible.

Reiterate to all kickoff attendees that they should be using active voice as they develop their proposal content.

Decide on your tone

The tone you take should vary depending on a number of criteria. In fact, tone can be described in many different ways using many different adjectives. Here are a few I tend to use most frequently:

- **Educational tone.** This is my general default, especially when I don't know all of the people who will be reviewing my proposal. When you take an educational tone, you do a lot more explaining. "We do this, and here's why," "We do that, and here's why," and of course, "Here's what this means to you."

- **Competitive tone.** In cases where someone else is the incumbent or you know the buyer prefers another vendor, consider writing with a more competitive tone. Take more opportunities, where appropriate, to differentiate between your solution and competitive solutions. You never want to sound too aggressive, but you don't want to be passive, either.

- **Conservative tone.** In cases where you are the incumbent and you know you are the preferred vendor, consider writing with a more conservative tone. You must still treat the opportunity like it's a new customer you're trying to win—not taking them for granted— just dial down the competitive language so you don't risk sounding too aggressive and, perhaps, coming off negative to the buyers who already know you.

- **Conciliatory tone.** I was involved in one procurement where the buyer went out to bid because their vendor, my client, totally screwed up. First, my client chose the wrong person to run the program. He was not well suited to that role. And then my client didn't genuinely listen to the customer's concerns when they called repeatedly to complain. When we wrote the executive introduction for the new RFP, therefore, we took a conciliatory tone. Not only did we take responsibility for our screw up, not only did we apologize, we tried to refocus them on the previous decades-long relationship where things had gone well.

As I mentioned, there are other 'tones' you can take. Regardless, just make certain that everyone in the meeting agrees to using the same one.

Include a benefit statement most of the time

One of the best ways you can make your proposal sound as though it was written by one person is to ensure each writer uses the same techniques. Specifically, make sure your team finishes most of their answers with some kind of benefit statement.

> *"The benefit to ACME is..."*
>
> *"The advantage you receive is..."*
>
> *"By implementing this approach, you get three things..."*

Whatever you do, whatever you decide, just make sure everyone who is involved in drafting content shares a mutual understanding of how to approach the writing effort.

8. What is it going to take for you to win?

OK, all the hard work is done. You've spent lots of time analyzing and reviewing, considering and arguing, and now everyone in your proposal kickoff meeting has a thorough and comprehensive understanding of what you're proposing, why you're proposing it, how to articulate it, and more. Following all this, there's only one more question to ask:

> What's it going to take to win?

I know, this sounds counterintuitive considering all of the work you've just completed, but it's not. Sometimes, oftentimes, it's not possible to see the big picture until you delve into the details.

Any writer will tell you that they can have a great outline, a great plan, but as they work drafting the content, as they dig into the details, they discover things they hadn't realized or appreciated at the beginning of the project. In the same way, the people who attend your kickoff meeting will discover things they hadn't realized before. They'll become enlightened.

So now, after everything else has been said, you need to stand up and ask in a soft, gentle voice, "what's it going to take to win?" Then stop talking and listen.

- Is anyone uncomfortable? You'll see it in their demeanor. Ask them what they're thinking.
- Is anyone hesitant? You'll see it in their demeanor. Get them talking.
- Are people excited and ready to get writing so they can win this? You'll see that, too. End the meeting so they can begin writing.

Just make sure you don't get angry or frustrated if someone isn't fully on board. It can be frustrating, but if you get angry, you'll just discourage people from contributing in the future. And that's a bad thing.

Phase 4:
Post-Proposal Selling

Your selling effort does not end when the proposal gets submitted. In many cases, it's only a temporary breather. In many cases, there's still more to do.

Do not neglect or minimize this step. Sometimes, with some buyers, everything that's come before is just a prologue to get you here.

15.

Presentation Development

Some RFPs are built around a single-step buying process while others have two or more. In a single step process, the buyer reviews and scores the proposals they receive and then selects the winner.

In other procurements, the buyer adds another step to the process; they review the proposals and then select two or three "semifinalists" who they invite to deliver an onsite presentation to decision makers.

This chapter includes a variety of best practices and a few tips related to post-proposal sales presentations.

ENSURING SALES MESSAGING CONTINUITY

One of the most important things any business development group can do to improve their proposal win rate is to maintain message continuity between their pre-RFP selling effort, their proposal, and their post-proposal presentations.

> The proposal you submit should be a continuation of the conversations the salesperson was having with the buyer prior to the RFP, and the presentation you deliver should be an extension of the messages you communicated in the proposal.

Unfortunately, this doesn't always happen.

Too often, the proposal team writes an effective proposal and the seller gets invited onsite to deliver a presentation. Then, inexplicably, the salesperson takes back control and dismisses the proposal development team with a terse, "Thanks for the help with the proposal, but I got it from here."

This practice is not uncommon, to be sure, but it's not a best practice. In fact, it doesn't even make sense. If the proposal advanced the opportunity to the short list, shouldn't the proposal team that wrote it be at least minimally involved in helping prepare the presentation? Common sense and an interest in continuity says they should.

The sales team and the proposal team should not be two separate groups working independently, they should be one integrated, unified team working together towards a common cause. This is not only the best practice, it ensures continuity of the sales message from the pre-RFP selling phase to the post-proposal presentation phase.

BUYERS WANT TO HEAR FROM OPERATIONS STAFF

If you submit a proposal and the buyer selects you to go onsite and present, remember that most buyers do not want a presentation from a salesperson. This is a bitter pill to swallow for many in the selling community, especially since it's the salesperson who got the opportunity started and has seen it through to this point.

Regardless, buyers almost always want to meet with and hear from the people who actually deliver the service they're buying.

- If they're buying payroll services, they want to hear from the account manager or payroll manager they'll be talking with when they submit their weekly payroll numbers, or the person they will actually be calling if they have issues or questions.
- If they're buying IT security software, they want to hear from someone who is an expert in IT security, who can explain with authority and granularity how your solution is going to solve their problems.
- If they're buying medical staffing services, they want to hear from the recruiter or recruiting manager who will actually be filling

open positions, and hear firsthand this person's familiarity with the market, the challenges in that market segment, and how they are ultimately going to deliver the results the buyer wants.

See the point? Salespeople are still responsible for orchestrating the whole thing, for bringing in all of the expert presenters, for managing the overall message and its delivery. But when actually delivering the presentation, the buyer wants to hear from and meet with the experts in your company who are delivering your service to them.

Let me be clear. The salesperson is still the conductor. You are still the first person to stand up, to coordinate the whole presentation, and to introduce all of the others. You're the quarterback. But buyers want to hear most from the people you brought with you.

Choosing your presenters

Putting your operations staff in front of buyers is smart, but just as important is choosing the best person for the job. Some people may be experts in their field, but they aren't necessarily good when they're in front of others. Leave these people back in the office where they can use their operations skills to do operations stuff. It's where they belong.

There are some experts, though, who excel in this outward facing role. They don't just come alive in front of other people, *they own it*. When they start talking about what they do, they exude confidence, they ooze credibility, and they inspire trust.

I was once in a meeting where a construction company was hosting a potential buyer. Various people took the podium to talk about their portion of the project, and it was all very pleasant with casual dialogue. Then a site manager got up, dressed in jeans, a little bit of mud still on his boots from a jobsite he just came from—*street creds*. From the moment he opened his mouth, he owned the room. Totally owned it. He oozed credibility. When one of the potential customers said, "We had hoped to do it this way," he began shaking his head and said "No you don't and here's why." The entire room was fully engaged, listening intently to every word he spoke. It was amazing.

You need to find *that guy*. He's the one you want presenting when you're down to the 11th hour and everything is on the line. He's the guy that will close the deal and surge you across the finish line.

HOW TO STRUCTURE YOUR PRESENTATION

In some cases, a buyer's invitation to present will be very structured and prescriptive. They may dictate the topics you need to address, the handouts you must provide with each topic, and even the time you can allot to each topic. In these instances, it's important to provide them exactly what they're asking for.

Despite how prescriptive they may be, though, do not forget to make your presentation about them. Give them the information they want, the way they want it, but always include those all-important benefit statements:

- *What this means to you is...*
- *The advantage to you is...*
- *This approach has many benefits, but the most important is...*
- *One of the things you said is important to you is X. With this approach, X is exactly what you get.*

Most other sellers are going to follow the buyer's instructions, and in the process, they're all going to sound the same, like a bunch of feature preachers. Against this cacophony of sameness, you are going to stand out because you've gone the extra step to make it about them.

Solution-focused presentation

Some buyers invite you to present, but they don't provide instructions. So instead of a fill-in-the-blank kind of question, it's more like a great big essay question; you get to choose what you're going to say. It is exactly these situations where many sellers tend to fall back on their seller-focused presentations, *here's who we are, here's what we do, us we me, us we me.*

When faced with an essay question kind of presentation, the best approach is to build a solution-focused presentation around what the buyer wants and how you're going to help them get it.

1. Restate what you understand they are trying to achieve

Begin your presentation by restating your understanding about what they want. Include both a list of the challenges that must be overcome along with the outcomes they want.

> When we receive an RFP, we don't just sit down and figure out how we're going to answer questions. That's what most companies do. What we do is we sit down as a team to review what you want. We discuss it, we analyze it, and we consider it from all angles. Only after that do we ask ourselves, "How can we solve this? What's it going to take to get them what they want?"
>
> So, to start our meeting today, I want to begin by reviewing what we understand you want.

However you word it, however you configure it, starting your presentation by focusing on them and what they want is ideal. It ensures they understand that you understand their issues and concerns and, ultimately, the outcomes they expect.

2. Overview of the solution you are proposing

Now you get to talk about yourself and the solution you're proposing. Keep your explanation at a fairly high level; it's never good to get bogged down in details too soon or too deeply. If you review a topic and nobody has questions, keep going. That topic is nothing they care too much about.

What is likely going to happen is you get to a topic they do care about, and then they'll stop you to ask questions. This is why it's so good to introduce each topic at a high level and to keep moving through your agenda; it saves time for the things they want to talk about in more depth.

3. Explain how your solution overcomes their challenges and delivers the desired outcomes

This part of your presentation may happen and probably should happen at the same time you are presenting your solution. I break it out separately because I want to highlight how important this step is to the overall success of your program.

You began your presentation by reviewing what they want to accomplish, then you described your solution. Now, you have to make certain that you link the two things together. Your solution means nothing to them if it doesn't help them get some outcome they want.

4. Explain how your solution is both different and better than competitive alternatives

We previously discussed the importance of differentiating your solution from competitive alternatives. This argument applies to your presentations just as much as it does to your proposals. In some respects, it's more important.

The buyer is actively evaluating, in person, each vendor. The buyer is actively considering the strengths and weaknesses of each. By making your case about why your solution is a better alternative, you're appealing to their reason at that critical point when they are most open to it.

> We understand you have more than a few qualified vendors to choose from. But we also understand there are differences between vendors. These differences are important because they can have a big impact on the outcomes you receive.
>
> Here are three reasons why the solution we are proposing will produce better outcomes for you than any other solution from any other vendor you may be considering...

If you make a compelling statement like this, if you have the courage to say exactly how your solution is different and better than what anyone else is offering, you will make an impact. You may not win, but you'll definitely make an impact.

PRESENTATION TIPS

In addition to everything else we've discussed in this chapter, following are a random smattering of tips and tricks I've collected over the years.

Gather intelligence beforehand

Before an RFP is published, sellers have free rein to call on buyers, to meet with them, get to know them, learn about their issues and interests, etc. After the RFP is published, though, sellers are severely restricted. Most RFPs include instructions that say something along the lines of, "You cannot speak with anyone in our organization about this RFP, *or else...*" The restriction usually comes with serious warnings and admonitions that sound ominous if not downright draconian: "If you break this rule, you will be removed from consideration, disallowed, admonished, penalized, and otherwise punished in the severest manner we are legally permitted to pursue." These harsh warnings are usually sufficient to discourage most sellers from reaching out to decision makers during the RFP process.

In my experience, though—*and there is admittedly some gray area here*—many buyers don't always enforce the "no contact" restriction into the post-proposal presentation stage of the process. In my experience, it's often permissible, or at least tolerated, for a seller to ask questions about a procurement before they go onsite to present.

> *Hi Tom. I can't tell you how happy we are that you invited us to present to your team. We've started preparing our presentation, and I have a few questions.*

In all the years I've been involved in sales and later in the proposal profession, I've only rarely had anyone push back against this reasonable request. This doesn't mean someone won't, and some have, but most recognize talking with you will provide a better and more focused presentation when you go onsite.

They can always say no. But if they agree, I have a few questions prepared.

- Is there something your team wants to learn more about?
- Is there something, in particular, your team liked about our proposal?
- Is there anything, in particular, your team didn't like about our proposal?
- Is there anything we wrote that needs clarification?

General questions are the best because they don't put people on guard. But if someone is friendly and wants to be helpful, they'll open up on their own.

Be prepared to abandon your presentation

I've always believed the best presentations are those where the buyer completely takes over by asking questions. In my mind, this means they're engaged and they're interested. There are things they want to know as they evaluate your solution.

When this happens, don't be stubborn. Don't stick to your script. Sit back, relax, and let them drive. The better you respond to what they care about, the more likely you're going to win the sale.

Make sure to finish presenting before your allotted time is complete

This is one of those statements that is so obvious, it doesn't need to be said out loud. Except it does.

Always, always, always make sure you are done speaking before your time is up. If they want to keep asking questions, stand there and keep answering. Remember, they can go past your allotted time, that's their right. Just make sure you don't.

Phase 5:
Post-Proposal Research and Analysis

In an earlier chapter, I said the difference between true professionals and perpetual rookies is their commitment to learning from past performance. Rookies don't spend much time reviewing their performance or analyzing their successes and losses. Professionals are different. Professionals take time to review their past performance and analyze their successes and losses. They learn from both.

This section of the book explores multiple ways that sellers can review, analyze, and learn from their past performance.

16.

Debrief Your Staff

Your business development team already know what's working and what's not. If you want to know, too, all you have to do is ask. If they feel safe from retribution, they'll share, and you'll learn.

How to ask

I recommend beginning each post procurement evaluation by interviewing your staff involved in the proposal development effort. This includes everyone on your team: salespeople, SMEs, proposal writers, and even the person who prints and assembles each proposal.

Make certain—*and this is critical*—to create a safe environment where they can speak freely, where they're safe from retribution. Then ask them for their honest opinions.

- What worked and what didn't?
- Which processes could work better? Which could be eliminated?
- Did you address the customer's problems or did you just talk about yourselves?
- Are SMEs truly available to proposal writers or are they too disconnected from the process?
- Is one person dominating the entire effort or are all encouraged to participate?
- Is the salesperson sufficiently informed to provide meaningful insights and intelligence?

These are just a few questions to get you started; you could easily come up with many more. Just take care not to make your interviews too structured. Let them flow where people want to take them. These are the things your employees care about most.

Your employees know a lot. Learn from them. All you have to do is ask, give them a safe place to answer, and then listen. You'll benefit from what you learn.

17.

Calculating Win Rates

Win rates are an excellent way to quantitatively measure the effectiveness of an organization's proposal program as it is today. After calculating a baseline, these metrics are also an excellent tool for measuring progress. After all, making changes to your existing processes are useless unless you can be certain the changes you've made result in better outcomes.

In general, I recommend calculating eight ratios:

- Gross win ratio.
- The short list and presentation win ratios.
- The incumbent and new business development ratios.
- The RFP response ratio.
- The shot in the dark proposal response and win ratios.

In addition to calculating these ratios for your overall business, I recommend calculating these ratios for each line of business, target market, or whatever other groupings make sense for your operation. For example, you may calculate the incumbent win ratio for your entire business, but then separately calculate the same ratio for the Western division and the Eastern division. This gives you a more granular and precise view of how well you're doing overall and in each region.

Gross win ratio

The gross win ratio is the most basic and fundamental of all RFP-related win rates. The Gross Win Ratio is calculated by dividing the total number of RFP opportunities you've won by the total number of RFPs to which you've responded. For example, if you responded to 100 RFPs and you won 20, then you divide 20 by 100 to come up with a win ratio of 20%.

This high-level ratio offers an easy way to measure the overall effectiveness of your proposal efforts. Its shortcoming, though, is it's too general to provide much actionable information. For example, if your Gross Win Ratio is 40% but all you've been doing is pursuing incumbent opportunities, I'd be concerned because 40% is lower than I'd expect. If your gross win rate is 40% but all you've been doing is pursuing new opportunities, then you're probably doing something right because, in this scenario, 40% is a good rate.

The point is the gross win rate may give you a big picture view, but it's too general to offer actionable intelligence. This is precisely why it is important to also calculate the incumbent and new opportunity ratios.

Incumbent and new opportunity ratios

Your win rate is going to vary dramatically based on whether you are the incumbent, or the competition trying to unseat the incumbent. If you are the incumbent, your win ratio should generally be higher—between 70% and 90%. If you are the competition, your win rate will likely be lower—between 5% and 15%, or between 30% and 40% if you're really good.

Therefore, if you want an accurate assessment of how well you are doing, more accurate than what is reflected in the gross win ratio alone, it is important to delineate between re-bids to existing clients and new bids to new clients.

- The incumbent ratio is calculated by dividing the number of opportunities you win from existing clients by the number of proposals you submit.

- The new client ratio is calculated by dividing the number of opportunities you win from new clients by the number of proposals you submit.

By distinguishing between incumbent opportunities and new business opportunities, you are able to build a much more accurate model of your overall business development performance.

Short list win ratio & presentation win ratio

In many industries, buyers who issue RFPs don't select vendors based solely on the proposals they submit but instead use a two-step selection process. In the first step, the buyer evaluates the proposals that are submitted by each vendor and selects the two or three they most prefer. In the second step, the preferred vendors are invited onsite to deliver a presentation to the people who will be making the ultimate buying decision.

Among people who respond to RFPs, this is often called "making it to the short list."

Understanding this process is important for any organization focused on improving the effectiveness of their proposal efforts. It means your overall success is not based solely on the quality or content of your proposal, it's also based in part on your ability to effectively present your solution in person.

I was contacted one day by a senior sales manager who wanted to arrange proposal training for her staff. Their win ratio, she explained, was far below what they thought it should have been. As we spent more time exploring their proposals and proposal process, however, it became clear the problem was not their proposals. In the majority of cases, the proposals they wrote were highly effective at advancing them to the short list. The problem we discovered was their presentations; their BD team was not effective at presenting their solution onsite. Said another way, they didn't need proposal training, they needed presentation skills training.

This story illustrates the importance of measuring your performance at a more granular level than what can be done with the gross win ratio, alone. By measuring performance at each stage of the process, you gain a more precise understanding of what you're doing well and what you might need to improve. This is precisely what the short list win ratio and the presentation win ratio are designed to capture.

- The short list ratio is calculated by dividing the number of times you make it to the short list divided by how many proposals you submit in response to RFPs. For example, if you submit 100 proposals and you advance to the short list 75 times, then you divide 75 by 100 to come up with a short list win ratio of 75%.

- The presentation win ratio is calculated by dividing the number of opportunities you win by the number of times you make it to the short list. For example, if you win 25 opportunities, and you made it to the short list 50 times, then you divide 25 by 50 to come up with a presentation win ratio of 50%.

Calculating the short list win ratio and the presentation win ratio gives you a much more precise understanding of what's working and what isn't.

RFP Response Ratio

I often work with managers who believe that every RFP represents an opportunity, and therefore, it's their responsibility to respond to each and every one they receive. I wholeheartedly, passionately, and without reservation, completely disagree with this approach. While it is true every RFP represents an opportunity, it's also true that not every opportunity is a good opportunity. Or a winnable opportunity.

Consider the case of a small, three-person web development firm. In the twelve months they've been in business, the three founders have racked up a noteworthy collection of clients and an impressive body of work. They've done an excellent job networking in the local business community, and people are starting to take notice of their fledgling firm. Then one day they receive an RFP, out of the blue, from a local but very large multinational corporation. The RFP describes a project that seems to be a great fit for what they do, but it involves developing and supporting a corporate-wide Web application that will be rolled out globally. Should they respond?

I've been in sales my whole life and, as a result, any opportunity I encounter gets my adrenaline pumping and my heart racing. Therefore, I'd probably make an effort to learn more about the opportunity, and specifically, why they chose to send the RFP to us. Barring some unusual findings, though, I would probably advise this client not to respond to this RFP for three reasons. First, all their customers to date have been local businesses under 250 employees. Their lack of experience working with a major multinational corporation is a significant hurdle that would be difficult to overcome. Second, they had no contact with this firm prior to receiving the RFP. The only information they have is what's presented in the RFP, and that generally isn't enough to thoroughly understand and qualify an opportunity. Third, with only three people in the firm, they lack the infrastructure that a major, multinational organization would certainly be looking for in an organization they will rely on to support a global application. Unless the three of them have nothing to do for the next few weeks and they're looking for something to pass the time, they have no business responding to this RFP.

As all of us know, though, business decisions aren't always so well-reasoned and logical. Bolstered by their recent successes, all they see when they look at this particular RFP is a huge opportunity, lots of dollar signs, and a shortcut to the big leagues. So they respond. Then they lose.

This story is entirely fictional, but it's not made up.

The purpose of the RFP response ratio is to measure how discriminating a company is in determining which RFPs to pursue. It's calculated by dividing the total number of RFPs that are pursued by the total number of RFPs that are received.

By itself, the RFP response ratio is not the most insightful piece of information you'll ever collect. If you respond to 100% of the RFPs you receive, for example, it could mean you aren't being very discriminating in how you use your resources. However, it could also mean that of the RFPs you've received, each was a good fit for your company. In other words, an optimal response ratio could be 50% for one business and 100% for another.

The value of the RFP response ratio is not the statistic itself; it's the awareness it creates among managers about how internal resources are being used. For managers who automatically respond to every RFP they receive, the RFP response ratio encourages them to invest time thinking about whether an individual RFP represents a legitimate opportunity that is winnable, or whether it's a poor fit that will more than likely result in a failed bid and much wasted time.

Shot in the dark ratios

Imagine you are standing in an open field in the middle of the night holding an official Daisy® Red Ryder BB gun (be careful, you'll shoot your eye out). Ten yards away, hidden in the inky darkness of night, there is a soda can resting atop a log. Your job is to shoot the can off the log. Emboldened by the feel of the cold steel in your hands, you raise the storied weapon to your shoulder, take careful aim as well as you can considering you can't see the target, and gently, confidently, you shoot. And you miss. And then the BB bounces back and hits you in the eye.

That's called a shot in the dark…and that is exactly what you do when you respond to an RFP that you get "out of the blue." You might get lucky every once in a while, but as often as not, you're just wasting resources responding to something you're never, or hardly ever, going to win.

There are two "shot in the dark" ratios you should calculate, the shot in the dark proposal response ratio and the shot in the dark win ratio.

Shot in the dark RESPONSE ratio

The shot in the dark response ratio gives insight into how often you chase surprise RFPs you receive "out of the blue." It is calculated by dividing the number of surprise RFPs you respond to by the number of surprise RFPs you receive.

Shot in the dark WIN ratio

The shot in the dark win ratio gives insight into how often you actually win a contract for surprise RFPs received "out of the blue." It is calculated by dividing the number of RFPs you respond to by the number of surprise RFPs you actually win.

The purpose of these shot in the dark ratios is to raise awareness among managers about how effectively they are using their resources and, in particular, if resources are being wasted pursuing opportunities when there's no realistic chance at winning.

OTHER WAYS TO CALCULATE WIN RATIOS

Calculating win ratios is a great way to gain insight into the effectiveness of your proposal effort, but you gain even more insight by adding more dimensions to the performance data you collect.

Segregating ratios by market or division

Many companies that offer an array of products or services will organize their sales efforts according to some criteria. It could be line of business, target market, geographic territory, etc.

Depending on the complexity of your organization and the volume of proposals you produce, it might make sense to go one step further and calculate each of the eight separate win ratios for each of the organizational units you've defined. For example, a technology company may have two divisions; one that targets government and another that targets commercial markets. In addition to calculating win ratios for the entire organization, this firm might gain far more insight into their proposal effectiveness by calculating separate win ratios for each market.

Adding revenue as another dimension

Suppose you respond to ten RFPs, and only win one. Your win rate is 10%. But also suppose the nine RFP opportunities you lost were each worth $10,000 while the one you won was worth $1,000,000. That makes a difference.

I prefer tracking win rates by opportunity. This gives you the best overall view of your business development efforts. But adding revenue into the calculation adds another dimension that can sometimes make the information you collect far more meaningful.

18.

Request copies of competitive proposals

If you are bidding on state and local government projects—*this does not apply to commercial projects*—you should always request copies of your competitors' proposals. It's a simple idea; if you have the opportunity to read their proposals, you gain insight into the message they're sharing with the buyer. You also learn what they think their competitive advantage is and, if you're lucky, how they're positioning themselves against you. Clearly, this is good information to have; it's the kind of intelligence that is actionable in future sales pursuits.

Many organizations don't request competitive proposals because they either don't know they can or they don't know how. In fact, you have a legal right to request copies of proposals from the federal government and in each of the 50 states. Further, most state agencies are so used to processing these requests they won't think twice about your request. It's normal and routine for them.

Background

Here's a brief background if you aren't already aware.

The federal government passed a law called the Freedom of Information Act, commonly referred to as FOIA. It allows anyone to request information from executive branch agencies. There are some limitations to what you can request. For example, they won't provide information that is confidential (they won't give you battle plans), private information on individuals (you can't request someone's personal tax return), etc. You can, however, request copies of proposals that vendors have submitted in response to RFPs.

The reason I'm introducing FOIA here is because it's a term sellers may hear from time to time, and it's often used colloquially whenever a company is requesting competitive proposals from a state agency: "*When we're done with this procurement, let's FOIA the other proposals to see what our competitors proposed.*"

Requesting state records

State and local government agencies (including schools that are publicly-funded) are not subject to FOIA. However, each U.S. state has its own open records laws that function essentially the same way. You can request all kinds of information—including proposals—just by asking and following their request guidelines.

Each state has its own process for requesting records. Contact each state's procurement website for more information. The National Freedom of Information Coalition is another good resource. They've done a good job compiling state procurement information to their website, nfoic.org.

You can limit what buyers share with your competitors

Though it's relatively easy to use open record laws to get copies of your competitors' proposals, some sections of their proposals may be redacted or not included in the package you receive. This is because state laws allow sellers to protect sensitive or proprietary content by labeling it confidential. This is precisely why most RFPs include verbiage that says something along the lines of, "The responder must indicate any section of this proposal that you consider confidential." If you request copies of all of the proposals submitted for a particular bid, you will typically receive everything except for the sections other sellers labeled as confidential.

Now turn this around. If you submit a proposal, but you do not label anything as confidential, your competitors will get everything, too—your pricing, contact information for your most talented and experienced employees, the recipe to your secret sauce, contact information for your best reference customers, etc.

Though you should leverage this privilege to protect the confidential and proprietary components of your bid, be reasonable. You can't get away with labeling your entire proposal as confidential, and most agencies will push back if you try to protect too much. In fact, it can even work to your detriment; if you claim everything is confidential, some courts may invalidate your claim leaving you with no protection. Therefore, make the effort to protect the important stuff that really does qualify as confidential and proprietary, but stop there. Depending on what you're selling, you may want to engage an attorney on this point to make sure you are doing it correctly.

ANALYZING OTHER VENDORS' PROPOSALS

In many respects, getting other vendors' proposals sent to you is the easy part. The hard part is figuring out what to do with them once you get them.

I recommend you do two things. First, name them and store them in some central location or drive so they're accessible by everyone. Second, assign someone to summarize those that are most relevant. Let's explore.

Summarize proposals and then share the summaries

When a company is writing a proposal in response to an RFP, they're typically trying to put their best foot forward, make the best possible impression, advance their most persuasive arguments. As a consequence, proposals typically represent some of the best competitive intelligence you're going to find—*anywhere*. In the sales world, getting access to a competitor's sales proposal is like finding a pot of gold. It only makes sense, then, to squeeze out every bit of knowledge and insight you can.

Here's the problem. If you give everyone in your business development organization—including salespeople, proposal writers, subject matter experts, and other managers—a stack of 100-page proposals, no one is going to read or analyze them. There's just too much work to do and not enough time to do it.

Therefore, I recommend you assign one astute, competitive-minded person to review and analyze the competitive proposals. This person's mission is to prepare a summary for each proposal. Each summary should be organized similarly so all reviewers get used to the same format. Organize your summaries in whatever way makes most sense to your business, but consider starting with these sections:

1. General summary of the overall effectiveness of the bid.
   1.1. Did it win the bid?
   1.2. Was it compelling?
2. Solution summary
   2.1. Describe the quality or effectiveness of the solution that was proposed.
   2.2. What features or capabilities do they write about that are relevant and our team should know about?
3. Proposal summary
   3.1. Is their proposal impressive? Weak? Average?
   3.2. Does their proposal look professional?
   3.3. Are there any techniques or concepts that we could use in our own proposals?
4. Strengths and weaknesses
   4.1. What specific strengths do they articulate?
   4.2. Are there any apparent weaknesses we can exploit?
5. Competitive assessment
   5.1. How do they position themselves in the market?
   5.2. How do they position themselves against us?
   5.3. Are they launching any new products or initiatives we should be aware of?
   5.4. Is there any evidence they ghosted our company or solution?
6. Opportunities to exploit
   6.1. Are there any apparent opportunities we may want to exploit in the future?
   6.2. Are there any ideas or concepts, or ways of expression, we might want to adopt?

6.3. Are there any people on their staff we may want to consider hiring if the need arises in the future?

6.4. Is there any new information about the buyer we didn't know before and that may be useful in the future?

6.5. In the references section, or in quotes throughout the body of the proposal, do they reference buyers from other agencies or companies? Do our salespeople know these people?

Again, you can organize your summaries in whatever way makes most sense to you, just make certain you standardize on one structure and stick with it.

Choose which proposals to summarize

Having access to unique summaries for each of your competitors' proposals would be awesome, but who has the time?

Therefore, spend time beforehand figuring out which procurements and proposals are critical and will generate the most insights. This way, you can learn from the intelligence you collect, but still minimize the investment you make in the effort.

Share your findings

In my experience, some companies that invest in this effort don't always do a great job sharing what they've found or make the best use of the information they uncover. I recommend you make a concerted effort to change that.

First, whenever a staff member completes a post RFP proposal summary, email the link to all of the people who were on the team responding to the proposal, as well as others in your company who may be interested in reading the information the review uncovered. This may include salespeople and sales managers, subject matter experts, proposal writers, program managers, company managers, etc.

Second, encourage the managers of each department—sales managers, proposal mangers, etc.—to raise the summary in their next staff or sales meeting, and discuss what their staff learned from the information. "Bob, what did you think of the summary of the XYZ procurement we got last week?"

The information gained is only valuable if people learn from it and, sometimes, the only way to get people to make the effort to learn from it is to challenge them to do it.

DOING A DEEP DIVE AGAINST A COMPETITIVE PROPOSAL

One of my customers was telling me about a competitive challenge his company was struggling with; they were placing second far too often whenever they were bidding against a particular vendor. Most of us have been in this situation at one time or another, but even if you haven't, it's easy to recognize how frustrating it would be.

What they decided to do was to perform an in-depth analysis comparing and contrasting their proposal against the competitor's proposal. They took it seriously, too, as evidenced by the time they invested in the effort.

First, they got a copy of the competitor's proposal. Then they commandeered a board room with two projectors. On one screen was their proposal and on the other screen was their competitor's proposal. He reported it took them a day and a half to complete the effort, but as a team, they reviewed each response to each question. They considered how each proposal was scored, they took notes about ways to improve their responses, and they identified areas in their proposal that were deficient.

Obviously, this sort of deep dive is time consuming, and it's probably not a process most small businesses could afford to do more than occasionally. Still, I can't imagine any other effort that would reveal as much understanding about your position relative to a specific competitor. Further, I can't help thinking how advantageous it would be for senior managers.

Senior managers aren't always involved in day-to-day selling efforts, so imagine if your company's senior managers have the opportunity to spend a couple days in a meeting reviewing exactly what your competitors are saying about themselves and their solution—*and about your company*. They'd see your strengths, to be sure, but they'd also see all of your warts and blemishes and shortcomings. It might be a great learning experience.

19.

Conduct Post-Decision Interviews with Buyers

Post RFP interviews, sometimes referred to as debriefs, are common in the federal world but they are relatively uncommon in commercial and non-federal government markets. In fact, I find it striking that, in the many years I've been in the proposal consulting field, I've worked with only a few companies who take the time and make the effort to debrief with the buyer following a procurement.

It is so striking because organizations that respond to RFPs on a regular basis can learn so very much by interviewing buyers after a procurement is concluded. You can learn what you did well, what you did not do well, whether your message was well received, their perception of your competitive position, and much more. For organizations serious about improving their proposal success rate, there are few methods that allow you to collect such marvelous insights as you can through buyer interviews.

Drafting a post-RFP interview

After an organization makes a commitment to conduct post-RFP customer interviews, the biggest challenge is often knowing what questions to ask. Because we spend so much time working on our proposal, our inclination is to focus our questions around the proposal. The problem is your customer doesn't only evaluate the way you've written your proposal, they evaluate the effectiveness of your solution, the price, the quality and appropriateness of the references you provide, the relevance of your experience to the current project, your credibility, etc. They also compare your overall offering to those being proposed by your competition. Said another way, if we consider the project from the customer's perspective, and we tailor our interview to reflect that, we're going to get a far more comprehensive and insightful understanding of our competitive position as well as the overall quality of our solution.

Before contacting any customer, therefore, it's important to draft a post-RFP survey that captures the most important and relevant information. I recommend drafting a master survey that includes both standard questions along with sections that are customized to reflect the specifics of each opportunity. Further, I recommend you organize your questions into five key areas: proposal effectiveness, solution effectiveness, price, your qualifications, and your competitive position.

Here is a list of sample questions you may choose to ask.

General questions

1. Please describe your overall impression of the solution we proposed.
2. Please describe your impression of how well our solution addressed your organization's needs.
3. Was there anything about our solution that you particularly liked?
4. Was there anything about our solution that you did not like?
5. Why did you choose <<name of the winning vendor>>?
6. Was there one thing, or multiple things, that counted for us (or against us)?

Price questions

1. Overall, did you perceive our price to be competitive?
2. Compared to other respondents, was our price among the lowest, among the highest, or somewhere in the middle?
3. Ultimately, how important was price to your decision?

Qualification questions

1. Your RFP listed a variety of qualifications and minimum requirements. In your view, how well did we satisfy these requirements?
2. Were there any specific instances in which we did not meet minimum requirements?

Competitive position questions

1. Did you rank respondent proposals? If so, where did we fall in that list? For example, did we come in #2, #3, or last place?
2. Our program is fully automated. Our competitors programs are either partially automated or completely manual. We worked hard in the proposal to emphasize this difference. Was this distinction clear to you? If so, was this distinction relevant to your decision process?
3. We understand you selected <<name of the winning vendor>>. Was it a difficult decision or were they the clear winner?
4. If a difficult decision, what were the issues you struggled with?
5. If they were the clear winner, what caused them to rise above the others?
6. We understand you selected <<name of the winning vendor>>, who had the contract previously. This is certainly common; most vendors choose the incumbent the majority of the time. My question to you is, under what circumstances would you have selected a new vendor over the incumbent? Was there something specific you were looking for? Was the case from other vendors just not compelling enough?

Proposal effectiveness questions

1. In general, what was your perception of our proposal?
2. Was there anything about our proposal you particularly liked?
3. Was there anything about our proposal you did not like?
4. Is there anything we can do in future proposals to improve them or make them more helpful to you?
5. You read a lot of proposals. We write a lot of proposals, and like everyone, we want to get better. Is there anything about the proposals you read—likes, dislikes, frustrations, aspirations—that you would change if you could?

I am not suggesting you use these questions; they're just examples to start the creative juices flowing. You should come up with your own list of standard questions. You can throw in a few questions that are opportunity specific, but make sure most of them are standardized. This way, you can compare your progress going forward.

Rules and guidelines about conducting a post-RFP interview

When you ask a buyer to participate in a post-RFP interview, there are a number of rules with which you must comply. Listed here are the most important.

Interviews, not questionnaires

I recommend scheduling interviews with buyers rather than sending them questionnaires to complete. There are three reasons for this. First, you are asking a buyer or client to invest their time in helping you to improve your proposal process. It's unprofessional to ask them to do all the work. Second, your response rate is going to be low if you do a questionnaire because, on their own, most people won't invest the time. Finally, you aren't going to capture the gems of information that you would otherwise get through an interactive interview.

When you are conducting an interview and the buyer says something interesting, interviews give you the freedom to explore those things in more depth...

> *"OK, this is great information, but I want to follow up to something you said. You said your team felt we didn't fully comply with your minimum requirements. Can you talk more about that? I'd like to understand where we fell short."*

The ability to follow-up a comment with another question is often necessary to get a full and comprehensive understanding.

Choose the right people to interview

If at all possible, it is best to interview the person in the buyer's organization who has senior, line management, decision making authority. Sometimes, you don't have that option; they let you talk with a contracting officer and that's all you get. Ask the question, though, and sometimes you'll get lucky.

Never argue

When the buyer answers a question, it is permissible to ask a clarifying question if you do not fully understand their answer or if you want to dig deeper. However, it is not permissible to argue. The purpose of this interview is to understand their perception of your proposal and your message, not to challenge the conclusions they've made. If you argue, you will necessarily put them on the defensive, and they will likely stop cooperating, or at the very least, the feedback they provide will be less than relevant.

Set the tone

When scheduling an interview, it's important to put the buyer at ease. One of the biggest concerns that most procurement people have, especially those associated with state or local governments, is that the seller will file a protest that challenges the fairness of a decision. If the buyer even suspects you might be looking for information to support a protest, the information you collect will be generic, nonspecific, and generally irrelevant. In contrast, if the buyer recognizes your primary goal is to improve the quality of the proposals you produce, to gain insight, then they will be more willing to provide meaningful and relevant feedback. There are always a few who will be reluctant, of course, but most of the people you talk with will be accommodating.

When scheduling an interview, therefore, I like to begin by making a clear statement:

> *Our purpose for requesting this interview is to improve the quality of the service we sell and the proposals we produce. We're trying to improve. Therefore, everything we discuss is "off the record."*

Most procurement people will be more willing to share their insights — honestly and openly — if you are open and honest with them about your intentions.

The caveat to this is you can't file a protest afterward, no matter what you learn. Make sure you're good with that before moving forward.

Choose your interviewers carefully

For larger organizations, I recommend hiring a management consulting firm, a market research firm, or a proposal consulting firm that has the capability to conduct client interviews on your behalf. Using a third-party firm can often produce better quality results because the buyer is not worried about offending the seller; they feel free to speak more openly.

While this approach is generally preferable, not every organization can afford to work with a third-party organization to perform post-RFP interviews. If this is you, that's OK. You can use inhouse staff and still collect a treasure trove of valuable and important information.

It is important to choose someone within your organization who has the skills and ability to perform a good interview. At a minimum, the person you choose must be personable and easy to talk with, familiar with the product or service you provide, familiar with the market including your competitors, and familiar with the types of problems and issues that your customers typically face.

In general, it is best if your interviewer is not the salesperson who has been working with the buyer, or the person who actually wrote the proposal. These people are generally too close to the opportunity to be objective, and more likely to take negative feedback personally. An objective, knowledgeable, third party will typically collect better and more meaningful information, and ask better follow up questions than someone who is too personally connected to the project.

Additional Selling Scenarios

In the interest of being thorough, there are other selling scenarios in addition to what's been described so far. These include handling recompetes when you are the incumbent, and handling RFPs you receive that you were not expecting.

20.

Recompetes When You Are the Incumbent

To thrive financially, most companies need to add new clients while also holding onto their existing clients. Everything we've talked about so far in this book has been about adding new clients. This chapter talks about pursuing recompetes to keep existing clients.

Recompetes explained

In most B2B and state or local government procurements, a contract for an ongoing program is awarded for a defined term. The initial term for recurring contracts is typically three years, and the buyer usually has an option to extend the contract for two one-year terms for a total of five years. The actual term varies based on the specific characteristics of each program, of course, but this is a common scenario.

As the end of the contract term approaches, the buyer is compelled to launch a new procurement effort to choose the next vendor. From an incumbent's perspective, this procurement is generally referred to as a recompete.

In the world of formal procurements, holding onto existing clients necessarily means you must have a great recompete program.

INCUMBENT VENDORS HAVE A BIG ADVANTAGE

Incumbent vendors have a distinct advantage over other vendors who are competing to win the business. There are three big reasons why.

1. **Familiarity**. Basic psychology says people like things they're familiar with. If I know you, if I've been working with you, if I'm comfortable with you, I'm more likely to continue working with you over someone else I'm unfamiliar with.

2. **Perception of risk**. "Better the devil you know than the devil you don't" is an age old saying that applies well to recompetes. The current vendor may not be perfect, but what if you bring in a new vendor and things actually get worse?

3. **Competing priorities**. Bringing on a new vendor to manage an existing program is a time-consuming venture. If I have the time to invest, I might consider new vendors. If the current vendor is doing well enough, but I'm up to my eyeballs in other high-priority projects, it's a no brainer; the current vendor is going to prevail.

For proof that incumbents have an advantage, you need look no further than your own win rates. If you calculate your incumbent win rates separate from your new business development win rates, as I recommended in a previous chapter, you'll discover your incumbent win rates are significantly higher. This all leads to one inescapable conclusion; incumbent vendors have a distinct advantage over other vendors who are competing to win the business.

Incumbents have an advantage, but...

Despite the inherent advantage incumbents may have, there are many circumstances where the advantage fades. Here are just a few:

- The incumbent is not doing a great job.
- The buyer hires a new internal manager or managers, and these new hires decide to reevaluate all current vendor contracts.
- The buyer is in between major projects or initiatives and has sufficient time to seriously consider other vendor alternatives.

- There's a change in general economic conditions that forces the buyer to reconsider what they're spending on the program.
- A competing vendor has read this book and, as a consequence, has been executing a highly effective pre-RFP selling effort that is getting noticed among the buying staff.
- Competing vendors offer better pricing programs and innovative services the incumbent does not.
- The buyer feels like the incumbent has become complacent and is taking them and their program "for granted."

Let's pause a moment and focus on that last bullet point. In my experience, sellers taking buyers for granted has resulted in the downfall of more incumbents than any other single factor. It happens when sellers believe, or start behaving like, their ongoing involvement is almost assured:

> We're already doing the work, right? We've got the systems in place, the people in place, we're meeting our obligations—everybody's happy, right? There's no way they're going to replace us, it would take too much work. Everybody relax, this is ours.

This attitude, common among vendors who have become complacent, is almost always fatal. It's fatal because buyers want you to take their programs seriously. They want you to work hard and endeavor to make their programs better, more efficient, and more responsive.

If a buyer gets the slightest inkling, the vaguest notion you are content to be on cruise control, milking the contract to maximize profits while eschewing opportunities to do better, *you're toast*. They'll turn the channel on you faster than a kid watching the evening news.

Bottom line: incumbents have an advantage most of the time, but sometimes they don't. Unless the buyer has specifically told you, "You are going to win this next procurement," which does sometimes happen, you cannot assume you are the preferred vendor. To the contrary, you must assume your future involvement is potentially at risk and the program you're managing could be awarded to another vendor.

The next logical question then becomes, "How do you increase the likelihood of winning more recompetes?"

HOW TO WIN MORE RECOMPETES

There are a number of things that sellers can do if they want to win more recompetes more consistently. Here are the most important.

1. Do a good job managing the current project

Yes, I know, it's so obvious it doesn't need to be said. Except it does.

If you want to keep an existing customer, you have to do a good job managing the program you've been assigned. If you aren't doing a good job, fix it. If you don't fix it, don't expect them to rehire you.

If you are doing a good job, it doesn't necessarily mean they're going to rehire you, but your chances are better than if you're doing a bad job.

2. Take each recompete seriously

If you want to win more recompetes more consistently, you cannot take them for granted. You need to take them seriously. The way to do this is to begin treating each recompete the same way you would treat any other opportunity you are trying to win.

> The most successful vendors pursue recompetes with the same effort and thoroughness they use to pursue new business opportunities where someone else is the incumbent.

I love this statement because it puts things in perspective. Your competitors are working hard to unseat you. You should be working just as hard to stay seated.

Admittedly, this statement is way short on specifics. Still, it's the right idea, the correct attitude, and a great starting point.

3. Treat each recompete as if it is a new contract

You should never treat a recompete as a continuation of the previous program, even though it may be. Instead, you should almost always treat a recompete as an entirely new procurement that has different or updated requirements and objectives. This is because, while many of the *requirements* and *specifications* may be the same or largely similar, others have changed. Even more important, and what you should pay special attention to, some of their *program objectives* may have changed. Consider this example.

The previous RFP emphasized a utilitarian solution; they wanted just the minimum services for the best possible price. Over the course of the contract, though, they began realizing the potential the program offers. So instead of utilitarian and low cost, the current procurement now emphasizes more services and better functionality resulting in better service for their customers.

See the point? If the new RFP is seeking different outcomes—more services and better functionality—you can't win the recompete by attempting to reuse your previous solution or your previous proposal, both of which were created with a utilitarian focus. It's a new procurement with new objectives, so it requires a new solution and a new proposal.

Do not try to reuse what worked before. Treat this procurement the way your competitors do, as a totally new procurement, and draft a new solution and a new proposal in response.

4. Engage business development staff

Building on the idea that you need to pursue each recompete as if it is a new opportunity, it only makes sense to engage your new business development team to help you win it. Let's explore.

NBD vs. AM

In the selling profession, there are generally two types of broadly-defined sales roles, new business development reps (NBD) and account managers (AM). While they are both in customer facing positions, their roles are very different—and so are the skills required to do them.

NBD reps are the hunters. Their job is to go out and find opportunities, develop them, and close them. Pursuing opportunities is their superpower.

Account managers are all about building relationships. Their job is to get to know the customer's staff, build strong relationships, identify problems that arise and solve them quickly, and in general, make sure the customer's staff is happy with the service they're receiving. Keeping existing customers happy is their superpower.

Both roles are necessary, even critical, but they're also very different. If the mission is to pursue and close a business opportunity, it only makes sense to rely on your NBD team to do it. It's what they do.

Admittedly, this is not a "new business" pursuit in the truest sense; you already won the business once. Still, treating it like it's a new opportunity by engaging an NBD team does two important things. First, it sends the correct message internally, that you aren't just skating along but investing the resources to win the recompete. Second, it sends the same message to buyers that you're taking the procurement seriously.

5. Recognize and exploit your real competitive advantage

If you are the incumbent, then your primary competitive advantage is your regular, everyday access to the customer's staff. This. Is. Huge. And if you don't believe me, ask your competitors. They would give almost anything to have the same access to the buyer you have every day.

Understand, this does not mean you can take advantage of the situation in a blatant way, using it to hype your products and such. You'll get shut down if you do.

But it does mean you can use your access to accomplish the subtle things like building strong personal relationships with their staff, exploring and understanding their internal problems that they'd never admit out in the open in an RFP, and learning the real, personal motives of the people who make or influence the procurement decisions.

The more you know them, the more they know you and have confidence in you, the more likely they'll find ways to keep you around when the recompete happens.

6. Recommend incremental improvements

As the incumbent vendor, you've learned a lot about day-to-day operations and how best to manage your customer's program. You've likely developed insights into what's working well, what's not working so well, and what changes you could make to produce better results for them. Armed with this knowledge *and* your subject matter expertise, ask yourself this question:

> If you were them, if this was your program, what would you do to make it better?

You asking this question is really important because, from a customer's perspective, they aren't just buying the product or service you are selling, they also want the benefit of your expertise. They want your insights. They want your advice.

If you can do something to make their program better, to help them get better outcomes, they're listening. It's the "value add" they hope all their vendors will provide.

Recommend minor, incremental changes for the current contract

One excellent way to add value is to recommend minor changes or tweaks that will in some way improve your customer's program today. The tweaks that work best are often small things that make their lives easier. Based on your involvement...

- Can you modify your invoices to make it easier for Tom in accounting to reconcile them?
- Can you update your report package so Sally gets everything she needs on one report rather than having to cross reference two separate reports?

To be clear, I am not suggesting you make any big changes that fall outside the scope of the contract. When you won the business and signed the contract, you agreed to a specific list of responsibilities. This is all you get paid for, and it's all you are obligated to deliver. Still, there is no downside and lots of potential upside if you can recommend incremental changes that make their lives easier.

The way you approach it is simple.

1. Ask your customer-facing staff to take notes about what's working well, what could be tweaked, and what things appear to be frustrating the customer's staff.
2. After you're a year or so into the contract, sit down with your staff and figure out ways to solve the issues you've identified.
3. Schedule a meeting with the customer's program manager and explain that you have identified some tweaks to improve the efficiency or effectiveness of the program.
4. At the meeting with the client, explain what you've found, the changes you'd like to implement, and then ask for their permission to go forward.

You don't have to follow this exact process, but I find it's generally easier for customers to process change if it's presented all at one time rather than piecemeal over time.

This incremental improvement effort is relatively simple, to be sure, but it demonstrates you are engaged in the program and want to make it successful. Buyers look favorably on vendors who are committed to their program's success.

7. Recommend major changes for renewal contracts

Recommending small, incremental changes is a great way to build goodwill during the term of the current contract, but let's go one step further and maybe score even more points by recommending substantial changes for the next contract they issue.

You are an expert in your field and you have other experts on staff. Knowing what you know about their program, and with your collective expertise, how would you change their program to give them more of what they want?

Think creatively about the options.

*   Is there a process you could make more efficient? More effective?

- Is there some practice you could change that would reduce their liability? Or improve responsiveness for their customers?
- Could they see significantly better results if they redefined their processes?
- Is there a portion of their system that you could automate or streamline?
- Is there an approach they're using that is not appropriate for the situation? Could it be made better if the customer used a different approach?
- Is their current project design approach overlooking an important consideration?
- Is there something they should consider that they haven't even thought of?

I appreciate these examples are somewhat vague, but hopefully you're seeing the point. As an expert in your field, you can look at their program and see opportunities for improvement. Sharing your expert insights can add significant value to your relationship.

> People buy from your company not just because of the services you provide but because of the expert advice and guidance you can offer.

There are a few things to remember when making recommendations about their program.

1. Schedule a meeting with senior decision makers

When proposing major changes to the next contract, it may work best to schedule a meeting between a relatively small group of leaders versus a larger team of operations staff. This does not mean you exclude the operations people totally or forever; it's just the operations staff can be averse to change because it often means more work for them. A senior decision maker is usually more open to change if they recognize it will produce benefit for the organization.

Timing wise, consider scheduling your meeting about six months before the program is due to be rebid. This will give the buyer ample time to consider and incorporate your recommendations into their new procurement.

2. Be clear about your purpose and recommendations

When requesting the meeting, it's important you be clear about your purpose and the recommendations you make:

> We've been managing your program over the last couple years. In that time, and with our expertise in this field, we've compiled a number of recommendations for you to consider when you rebid this contract.
>
> If implemented, we anticipate these recommendations will make invoice reconciliation easier for your staff, improve responsiveness to your customers, and over a three-year term, reduce your program costs by about 10%.

When you ultimately meet and present your recommendations, state them clearly in a bulleted list. Go easy on the detail. The purpose of the meeting is for you to present each recommendation, one by one, and explain how it will benefit them if they adopt it. All the specifics can be worked out later.

The more they see you as a consultant, as a value add to the service they're already buying, the more favorable your position when the recompete ultimately happens.

21.

How to Handle RFPs You Weren't Expecting

If you've been reading sequentially, you already know the best practice is to build a proactive selling process, one in which you "make the sale" long before the RFP is issued. Despite this, despite all of your careful planning and proactive efforts, you are inevitably going to receive a surprise RFP, one you receive 'out of the blue' that you are neither expecting nor are prepared for. What do you do?

Understanding your chances

Before you take out a pencil and start scribbling your response, remember that your chances of winning a surprise RFP are low. Single digits low. It's difficult to get exact figures because most private organizations do not publish or share their win rate statistics or the unique business practices on which those statistics are based. Still, based on my experience and the experiences of other proposal professionals I know, the average win rate for "out of the blue" proposals is almost always in the low single digits.

Accepting your chances at winning are in the low single digits, take a moment to ask and then answer these two questions:

- Is it worth the investment in staff time and money it's going to take to draft a proposal knowing you're likely going to lose?
- Is it worth the opportunity cost—the time this proposal will steal from other more winnable opportunities?

If you're like many salespeople, these two questions might not even slow you down; your inclination is to barrel ahead undeterred. If so, at least take the time to apply some discipline to your decision *before* you respond.

Apply some discipline to your decision process

The best way to make a good bid/no bid decision is to apply at least some structure to your process before you put pencil to paper. This usually involves addressing these two topics:

1. Evaluate your situation
2. Consider your options

Like most things in life, a little bit of planning and forethought goes a long way, even with RFPs received out of the blue.

EVALUATE YOUR SITUATION

To better evaluate your situation, take some time and answer these four questions.

1. Have you had any substantive conversations with the buyer about this opportunity before the RFP?

If you have not had any substantive conversations with a decision maker about this program, then all you know is what they say in the RFP—and that's not very much. You do not know about the competition, what the buyer thinks of the competition, if any of the decision makers already have vendor preferences or have made vendor decisions, what their pain points are, etc. You are going in blind.

Maybe you were expecting the RFP but just not today. You've had previous substantive conversations with one or more decision makers about their program. Based on these conversations, you know something about the decision maker's personal interests and objectives, background about their program, etc. This improves your odds. Still, remember that despite these conversations, you still didn't know the RFP was coming out today. This suggests there's something going on in the background you don't know about.

One more thing. When I use the term "substantive conversations," I'm talking about conversations with decision makers. Procurement people and contracting staff don't count because, generally, they aren't decision makers. They may be involved in the process, even leading the process, but they don't generally make the purchase decision.

Decisions are usually left up to operations or program staff, or to staff who have been conscripted onto a proposal review committee. A contracting officer telling you your product is "exactly what they're looking for" is not a substantive conversation.

2. Do you have history with the buyer? How well do they know you?

One of my clients was working with the Eastern division of a large organization when they got an RFP from the Western division for the same service. No one had ever talked with anyone in the Western division, so this RFP really was 'out of the blue.' We did have the good sense, though, to call some of our contacts in the Eastern division to see if we could learn more.

In this case, the program manager in the Western division called the program manager in the Eastern division, and asked him all about our service. We got a good recommendation from our contact.

The point here is even though we didn't talk to the Western program manager, they still learned about us from someone within their own company. I wish we would have known more, but based on these circumstances, pursuing this RFP seemed like the best move.

3. Is the product or service they want to procure well-aligned with the service you provide?

Do you already sell what they want or will you have to build something to provide the service they require?

Generally, buyers don't want to be your test pilot, a hapless victim of your learning curve. They generally prefer to buy a product that has already been implemented and is in production somewhere else.

If you do not have the product they want, already in production, this is a red flag. Think carefully before proceeding.

4. Is this a new procurement or is there an incumbent vendor?

It's tough to unseat an incumbent vendor. That's not to say it doesn't happen, but it's not easy. Generally, unseating an incumbent requires a major sales effort prior to the RFP, and a buyer who is convinced that switching to a new vendor offers more benefits than the risk it introduces. This only happens when they see you as credible, and that only happens when you invest time establishing your credibility.

If it's a new procurement, your odds are better. It's easier to win a new procurement than it is to unseat an incumbent vendor. Still, they've probably been talking to another vendor, or to other peers who work with another vendor, so that vendor has the upper hand.

By taking the time to evaluate your situation, to consider what you know and what you don't, to ponder what you're up against, you'll be in a better position to make an informed decision.

CONSIDER YOUR OPTIONS

Before deciding to respond or walk away, it might also be worthwhile to take some time and consider all of your options.

Option #1: Reach out to the contact

RFPs almost always include admonitions that you cannot speak with anyone in the buyer's organization during the course of the procurement.

They usually list a contact person, typically a procurement staff member or a contracting officer, to whom you can submit questions.

It's important to understand this contact may know something about the program going out to bid, but not always, and generally not very much. Further, like I mentioned previously, the procurement person generally is not involved in making a purchase decision. Despite all that, with little else to hang your hat on, the procurement person can be a source of information...*but only if approached carefully.*

How to ask procurement officers for information

First, recognize that procurement people are interested and motivated to make certain every procurement is a competitive procurement. When asking for information, therefore, the trick is to tie your request to their motivation. If you call and say, "I'd like to ask some questions about the program," they'll reply with their standard response: "Put it in writing." Then they'll answer your questions, if they choose to, and share those answers with all bidders. Clearly, this doesn't help us.

However, if you turn it around and articulate it like I've done in the following passage, you're framing the conversation; you're making them the salesperson trying to convince you to participate:

> *Hi Paul, we received your RFP. Thank you for including us.*
>
> *We're trying to decide whether or not we should respond. See, we've never talked with anyone at your organization before, and we don't know anything about the program. I'd like to ask a few general questions to get some background.*

It's that first statement that's so important: *"We're trying to decide whether or not we should respond."* Now Paul is thinking to himself that he needs to engage you and convince you to respond. Remember, one of his goals is to make this a competitive procurement.

This approach doesn't always work. Some procurement staff will shut you down like you're a kid asking for dessert before dinner, "no that's against the rules and it's unfair to the other bidders." Still others will reply, with some hesitation, "sure, I can answer a few questions."

If you get this far, be prepared with some basic, non-threatening questions, just enough to get the conversation started.

1. From reading the RFP, it appears this is an ongoing program, so I assume you put it out to bid every few years. Is that correct?
2. So the last time this program was put out for bid, it was about three years ago?
3. Who is the current vendor?
4. How long have you been working with them?

I'm not asking any super deep questions, or anything that should make him uncomfortable, just some high-level background. Still, if I get through just these four questions, I've already learned a lot.

First, I've learned if this procurement is going out on schedule, or if it's going out ahead of schedule. On schedule tells me they're issuing the bid because they have to, not necessarily because they want to. If it's going out ahead of schedule, if it's only been two years since the last RFP, for example, I know something's going on that's causing them to bid early. Nobody bids early unless there's a compelling reason why. So I might even ask a follow up question to clarify, "Why are you going out to bid early?" If it's going out behind schedule, it's been five years instead of three years, they're probably happy with their current vendor, and have issued a couple extensions to the current contract.

Second, I learned who the current vendor is. If I'm in tune with my market, if I've been paying attention to my win/loss record, I know who we compete well against and who we compete poorly against. Either way, it's good information.

Third, I learned how long they've been with their current vendor. If they've been with that vendor for a long time, it's going to be a lot harder to replace them.

Obviously, what you may learn from this effort hardly constitutes a comprehensive dossier, but at least I've learned a few things that will help me decide whether to pursue it.

What if the procurement person is cooperative?

One more thing. If your call is going well and the person is being cooperative, get as much as you can and then consider asking to speak with the program manager. Explain your request by saying, "the more I know about the program manager's interests, the better I'll be able to target exactly what it is they want when we configure our proposal."

Most of the time, you get denied and the call stops there. There are those occasions, though, where a forward-looking company will accommodate your request and set up a phone meeting. Not often, but it does happen.

To be clear, this is more likely to happen when the buyer is a business but almost never when the buyer is a state or local government organization. The difference is businesses are guided by internally-created procurement rules while state and local government procurements are guided by laws and regulations. Some businesspeople are willing to push the rules if they're interested in what you're selling, but most government people would never consider risking it.

Option #2: Consider partnering with another vendor who is in a better position

In some cases, you may consider partnering with a competing organization to provide some component of the solution they propose. For example, suppose the buyer wants a service organization with support offices in six major cities. You already have support offices in two of those cities out West, and one of your competitors has support offices in four of those cities out East. Separately, neither of you meet the minimum program requirements. Together, though, you could provide a more comprehensive solution than what either of you could propose separately.

When two organizations build this kind of alliance, one is usually the prime contractor and the other is a subcontractor. You have to decide which is best suited to be the prime, and you also have to decide whether you can work with the other business.

While this approach is not used as often in the B2B world, it's common in federal government contracting. In fact, it's one of the best ways that businesses new to the federal sector—who would otherwise never be considered for a federal contract—begin developing experience, a reputation, a list of references, and industry relationships.

Option #3: Decline to pursue but leave the door open

If you receive an RFP out of the blue, and you have no relationships or history with the buyer, no inside contacts to guide you, and it represents little more than a shot in the dark, you may consider declining to respond. This is a perfectly acceptable thing to do, and in fact, is often the wisest thing to do.

If you decide to decline, though, make sure you notify the contact who issued the RFP. First, send an email or a letter notifying them that you won't be able to respond, but request they keep you on their bid list. Make it clear that you'd like to bid the next time they publish the RFP for this program. This ensures you keep your future options open.

Second, follow up with a phone call to verbally thank them for including your company in the bidders list. You may also offer some kind of explanation why you aren't responding.

> *We are in the process of implementing two new clients, and our best resources are stretched thin. We would like to work with you in the future, though, and we would love to be on your bidders list the next time this program goes out to bid.*

Depending on how the call is going, you might also see if you can learn more about their program. For example, if you don't know it, find out who their current vendor is.

Option #4: Pursue it

Even though your chances of winning are low, there may be some good reasons to pursue an out of the blue RFP.

It's a uniquely perfect fit for what you do

I almost hesitate to include this as a reason to pursue a surprise RFP because, too often, sellers use this reason as a justification to pursue almost every RFP that comes in the door. Despite this, there are some times when an RFP is legitimately a perfect fit for what you. Therefore, even though you didn't know about the RFP beforehand, if you sell exactly what they say they want, AND you can make a compelling case the solution you offer is both different and better than competitive alternatives, responding with a proposal might be a bet worth making.

It's one of your targeted accounts

The RFP is from an organization you included on your targeted account list, even though you haven't begun calling on them yet. So while you probably won't win this particular procurement, responding with a proposal might be a great way to start the conversation. In cases like this, I recommend making your proposal very educational, with an unusually large number of case studies and quotes from your other happy customers.

In a very real sense, treat it almost like a marketing document than a proposal; use it as a tool to launch a conversation after this procurement is completed.

It's a division of a company you already work with

If you already work with one division of a company, and you received a surprise RFP from another division, I almost always respond to those unless we are clearly unqualified. Many times, you will learn that while you haven't been talking with the buyer, they've been talking amongst themselves.

Political reasons

Sometimes, it happens that a higher up in your company instructs you to respond, even though everyone on your team knows you're going to lose. I hate it when this happens because it's such an irresponsible waste of organizational resources, but it happens all the time.

Shake your head, grumble under your voice, and start writing. This is one instance where your proposal truly is not a sales opportunity to win; it's a writing project to complete—*as quickly and efficiently as possible.* Grumble, grumble.

SCHEDULE A 'STREAMLINED' KICKOFF MEETING

You've made the decision to respond. Good for you. Now what?

First, do not do what far too many sellers do; simply roll up their sleeves and start copying and pasting content from previously written proposals. This is a common practice, but it's a worst practice, not a best practice, and it doesn't work.

The best practice is to initiate the same disciplined approach I outlined in the section titled, *Phase 3: Proposal planning and development*. This phase includes four unique parts described in four separate chapters:

- Scrutinizing the RFP.
- Proposal Kickoff Meeting Part 1: Compiling and Analyzing What You've Learned.
- Proposal Kickoff Meeting Part 2: Configuring Your Solution.
- Proposal Kickoff Meeting Part 3: Configuring Your Sales Message.

I understand this involved proposal planning effort is designed for opportunities that you've been pursuing for 12-24 months, not RFPs you receive out of the blue. This necessarily means there will be a lot of items you cannot address.

Despite that, working through the process, addressing as many items as you can and as many questions as you can answer, will produce better results. It may be frustrating in parts, but it will also impose the thoughtful consideration needed to help you build a better, more customer-focused solution and proposal.

Reference

Glossary

Some of the definitions listed here were referenced in this book. Others are terms that, while not specifically used in this book, you might hear when working with or around proposal and business development people.

11ᵗʰ hour decision maker

The 11th hour decision maker is a derogatory term for a senior manager who can never find time to participate in proposal strategy meetings when a proposal is being developed. Instead, this short-sighted manager waits until the proposal team has a response almost completed, and then they swoop in at the 11th hour to see what's being proposed and to make changes—often big, complicated changes that fundamentally alter the solution and dramatically impact content throughout the proposal.

Don't be an 11th hour decision maker. You're not helping anyone, you're making things worse not better, and nobody likes you.

AEC industry

AEC is an abbreviation for architecture, engineering, and construction. This industry relies heavily on RFPs and proposals to transact business.

Association of Proposal Management Professionals (APMP)

The Association of Proposal Management Professionals, APMP, is a professional organization dedicated to the business of proposals. An international organization with chapters in many countries and regions, they offer certifications to proposal practitioners as they practice their profession.

Capture management

Opportunity management is a term often used by B2B salespeople to describe their approach and plan to win an opportunity. Capture management describes a comparable function. It is most often used by federal contractors to describe their approach and plan to win federal government opportunities.

Chunking

Chunking is proposal industry jargon sometimes used by proposal professionals. It refers to editing a large, uninterrupted section of text into smaller chunks, each of which is preceded by a bold heading. For a typical business person who favors skimming your proposal rather than reading it, chunking dramatically improves readability. See *Skimmability*.

Color teams

Federal government contractors often rely on "color teams" to perform reviews at various stages of the proposal development process. A blue team, for example, is focused on reviewing the proposal's outline structure. The pink team, in contrast, is focused on the content that's been added to the outline. Then there's the red team, the green team, the gold team, the white team, and any other sub-process team colors you care to invent. Chartreuse? Vermillion? Puce?

Color team reviews make sense for many larger organizations that run sophisticated business and proposal development operations. In these environments, color team reviews are a best practice.

I've never fully embraced this color-coded system. It's partly because I'm colorblind; I always seem to show up at the wrong meeting. Aside from that, this multi-team approach is too involved for most small and midsize businesses to implement. Most lack the resources for such a sophisticated process.

Whatever review process you decide to use, regardless of whether it uses colors, make sure it is both right-sized and fully "implementable" for your business.

Column fodder

When buying organizations launch a procurement, they often know from the outset the one or two vendors they are most likely going to select. Still, contracting staff want the procurement to at least appear competitive because corporate rules or government regulations require it. Therefore, in an effort to stimulate competition, they encourage other vendors to bid, even vendors they've never talked with and know nothing about. They might even tell you your product "looks like a perfect fit" for what they're buying. Don't buy into this argument.

The truth is you probably don't have a chance at winning because they've already narrowed the field down to a few familiar vendors that don't include you. In fact, the only reason they talk to you nicely and act as though you have a chance at winning is because, more than anything, they want you to write a proposal in response to their RFP. If you do, you're providing them a valuable service; you're filling up another column in their vendor spreadsheet so they can report to their managers that the procurement is competitive. This is the definition of column fodder.

When this happens to you, you've officially been column foddered. I know, it sounds dirty. It feels dirty, too. But when you realize that most business development people have also been column foddered before, some repeatedly, you start feeling better about yourself.

Formal procurement

A formal procurement is a method organizations use for procuring goods and services that are expensive, strategically important, or high profile. In most cases, an organization will convene a group or committee responsible for documenting requirements or specifications for the product or service being acquired, draft a solicitation (typically a request for proposal), and then review the vendor proposals that are submitted in response.

Formal procurements take all the fun out of buying stuff, but major organizations maintain they result in better purchase decisions.

Ghosting (the competition)

"Ghosting the competition" is proposal industry jargon. Ghosting is a competitive tactic to take advantage of a competitor's weakness. For example, if you are pursuing a contract and you know your biggest competitor is in chapter 11 bankruptcy reorganization, you might ghost them by saying something like this: "Unlike some vendors in this market who are struggling with debt and financial issues as they try to reorganize, our company continues to be financially strong, consistently profitable, and debt free."

You have to be careful when ghosting the competition; you don't want to sound arrogant, boastful, or mean. Still, most buyers want to know where you're better and, especially, if another vendor is weak or struggling.

Gross win ratio

The gross win ratio offers an easy way to measure the overall effectiveness of your proposal efforts. While it's too general to offer in-depth understanding, it's a simple and easy way to measure overall progress going forward.

The gross win ratio is calculated by dividing the total number of RFP opportunities you've won by the total number of RFPs to which you've responded. For example, if you responded to 100 RFPs and you won 60, then you divide 60 by 100 to come up with a win ratio of .6, or 60%.

IDIQ (indefinite delivery, indefinite quantity)

IDIQ stands for *indefinite delivery, indefinite quantity*. It is a kind of contract that organizations use when they want to buy goods or services, they don't know exactly how much they will be buying, but they still want to get a negotiated rate. For example, suppose an organization buys office copier paper for 50 offices over a five-state region. They could have someone run down to the corner office supply store each time they need more paper, but they'd be paying full retail each time. As an alternative, they may negotiate an IDIQ contract at a better-than-retail price. Even though they don't know exactly how much paper they'll need, they know they'll need a good amount, they know how much they used last year, so why not get a better price?

Informal procurement

An informal procurement is a buying process that organizations use when the procurement does not exceed a particular price or the product being acquired is not strategically important. Depending on the organization, it may still require that certain procurement rules be followed, or that the buyer seeks bids from more than one company, but it's nowhere near as complex or structured as a formal procurement involving an RFP.

Kickoff meeting

A well-designed kickoff meeting has two fundamental components; an administrative function and a sales strategy function.

The administrative portion of the meeting includes everything typically included in a traditional proposal kickoff meeting: creating and publishing a proposal development schedule and firm deadlines, assigning RFP sections or individual questions to various writers, deciding what research must still be done and assigning those tasks to staff members, etc.

The sales strategy function is itself twofold; it involves figuring out what it's going to take to win, and then making sure all team members share that understanding. The sales strategy portion of the meeting should dominate the majority of the time you allot to your meeting and planning effort. That's because while assigning administrative tasks is *important*, a targeted, customer-focused sales strategy is *critical*. Indeed, the project's success or failure hinges on how well you complete this step.

Presentation win ratio

Many procurements are organized into multiple steps. For example, the buyer may evaluate the proposals that are submitted by each vendor, and then they choose two or three vendors they want to investigate further. These sellers are typically invited onsite to deliver a presentation to the people who will be making the ultimate buying decision. This is often called "making it to the short list" or being "shortlisted."

The presentation win ratio measures the effectiveness of your onsite presentations. If you are invited to present 10 times, and you win a contract or advance to the next step five times, then your presentation win ratio is 50%.

Prime contractor

To compete effectively, a vendor may sometimes partner with another vendor so, together, they offer a solution that meets the minimum qualifications. In these cases, one vendor will be the prime contractor and other vendors will be subcontractors. The prime contractor is the organization that signs the contract with the seller and is ultimately responsible for delivering the product or service.

Probability of winning (PWIN)

Probability of winning, or PWIN, is a calculation designed to give sellers insight into their chances of winning a particular procurement. PWIN can be calculated many different ways, from manual and entirely subjective reviews to highly sophisticated programs that calculate PWIN based on key performance indicators (KPIs).

Most small to medium-sized businesses don't have the resources to invest in sophisticated PWIN systems to guide their decisions. Besides, in many organizations, the decision to proceed is often based more on political considerations or the force of someone's personality than on objective data.

Still, if the managers can at least do a basic review of an opportunity before anyone begins writing, they may save themselves lots of time by walking away from opportunities they likely won't win.

Protest

A protest is a formal objection submitted by a seller to a government buyer when the seller believes a procurement has been awarded incorrectly because it violates laws or regulations, didn't follow the rules, or is in some way unfair. There are different justifications for submitting protests, so you have to understand the applicable laws and regulations before submitting the protest. This is why serious sellers will often work with attorneys to prepare their protests.

Too often, protests are being submitted these days not because the buyer did something wrong but because the seller is a sore loser and doesn't like that their competitor won instead of them. These protests almost never win, they might give the protester a bad name, and they muddy the water for the rest of us when we actually have a legitimate protest.

Qualifying (an opportunity)

A salesperson can easily waste a significant amount of time and resources pursuing a sales opportunity that is "not a good fit" for the product or service they're selling. Therefore, all professional salespeople are taught to "qualify" sales opportunities.

Qualifying a sale means the salesperson and sales manager go through a process whereby they evaluate the merits of the new opportunity against some objective criteria they've already established. For example, a seller might determine, for an opportunity to be well-qualified, it must meet the following criteria:

- It must involve a financial commitment above $500,000.
- The primary contact person must be director level or above with budget authority.
- The buyer must be interested in blue copiers rather than red.
- The opportunity is ideal if they're currently working with Dave's Fictional Copier Company, but it's still a favorable opportunity if they're currently working with Donna's Fictional Copier Company.

Ironically, many salespeople know how to qualify opportunities, but they fail to apply the same discipline to RFPs that they would apply to any other sales opportunity they encounter. In other words, they get an RFP in the door and, almost by default, choose to respond to the RFP—*even though they know nothing about the opportunity*. This approach is not only undisciplined, it generally wastes lots of resources.

Recurring contracts

A recurring contract involves an ongoing program that is periodically rebid. The way it typically works is an RFP is issued, vendors respond with proposals, and a vendor is then chosen to provide the goods or services. After a set period of time—usually three to five years—the recurring contract goes back out to bid and the process starts all over again.

Request for proposal

A request for proposal (RFP) is a formal document, published by a company or government entity, that requests vendors submit structured proposals in response to a list of specifications, requirements, or questions.

RFPs are generally far longer than they need to be, poorly organized, lack clarity, and almost always mandate unreasonable requirements and unreasonable response timeframes. Further, it's not uncommon for some RFPs to be issued immediately prior to a national holiday and mandate response due dates immediately after the same holiday.

It's a little known fact outside the proposal community, but true nevertheless, that Dante created a special place in hell—between the third circle (gluttony) and fourth circle (greed)—for procurement officers who set proposal due dates within a week following a national holiday.

Request for information

A request for information (RFI) is a formal document, published by a company or government entity, that requests vendors submit structured documents in response to a list of questions.

RFIs are often used before RFPs. Buyers use them to learn about features or capabilities they may want to incorporate into their procurements and, in some cases, to exclude certain vendors who do not meet minimum qualifications.

Request for qualifications

In some industries, the engineering field in particular, a request for qualifications (RFQ) is almost identical to an RFP; it describes a project, lists the specifications, and asks respondents to submit a proposal in response. Despite the difference in naming, you still respond with a proposal and you still have to be customer-focused and persuasive.

Request for quote

A request for quote (RFQ) is a solicitation where a buyer requests the vendor respond with a quote for a particular product or service.

RFQ

An RFQ can refer to either a 'request for qualifications,' or a 'request for quote.' A request for qualifications is much like an RFP, and is most commonly used in engineering fields. A request for quote is a request for a firm price quote for a specific product or service.

Shortlist

Some procurements use a two-step process. After reviewing all of the proposals submitted (the first step), the buyer may choose two or three vendors who are invited onsite to conduct a presentation to decision makers (the second step). In the world of formal procurements, this is commonly referred to as 'advancing to the shortlist.' Presumably, whichever vendor makes the best presentation wins.

Short list win ratio

Many procurements are organized into multiple steps. For example, the buyer may evaluate the proposals that are submitted by each vendor, and then choose two or three they want to investigate further. This is often called, "making it to the short list." The two or three sellers who make it to the short list are typically invited onsite to deliver a presentation to the people who will be making the ultimate buying decision.

The short list win ratio offers insight into the effectiveness of your proposals. It is calculated by dividing the number of times you make it to the short list divided by how many proposals you submit in response to RFPs. For example, if you submit 100 proposals, and you advance to the short list seventy-five times, then you divide seventy-five by 100 to come up with a short list win ratio of 75%.

Skimmability

Skimmability refers to how well a section of text can be quickly skimmed by a busy reviewer who lacks the time or motivation to read the entire proposal document. A good skimmability quotient means your document is easy to skim and will be well-received by most reviewers. A poor skimmability quotient means no one is going to spend any time looking at your proposal. Sorry.

SLED

SLED is an abbreviation for State and Local government agencies and EDucational organizations. SLED organizations typically rely heavily on formal procurements to acquire goods and services.

SME

Abbreviation for "subject matter expert."

Sole-source

In situations where only one business can provide the product or service being sought, a government entity can seek a sole-source procurement. This means the buyer can award the contract to the seller while avoiding the traditional competitive bidding process. A lot of sellers seek sole-source procurements because it makes life so much easier, but few qualify.

Solicited proposal

A solicited proposal is a proposal document written in response to a formal solicitation, and can take the form of a request for proposal (RFP), request for information (RFI), request for quote (RFQ), or request for qualifications (RFQ).

In some cases, it may also refer to a marriage proposal solicited by a shotgun-toting father after learning his daughter is pregnant.

Subcontractor

A vendor may sometimes partner with another vendor so, together, they offer a solution that meets the minimum qualifications of a particular procurement. The prime contractor is the organization that signs the contract with the seller and is ultimately responsible for delivering the product or service. A subcontractor signs a contract with the prime contractor, and provides a subset of the overall product or service.

Subject matter expert

A subject matter expert, commonly abbreviated SME, is a person who has expertise in a particular subject or area. An SME can be a recognized industry expert, but a person does not necessarily need an advanced degree or certification to be considered an SME. For example, an accounting clerk who has experience integrating the seller's invoicing system with external accounting programs might be considered an SME because he or she has expertise in a particular area and can assist meaningfully in proposal development.

Despite this generally accepted definition, some members of the proposal community insist the abbreviation actually stands for, "Some May be Experts." This implies some may not be experts, and don't contribute that much to the process, but they pretend to be experts since it offers them higher pay and prestige as if they were actual experts. See *11th hour decision maker*.

Thud Factor

Conceived and made famous by author and proposal authority Dr. Tom Sant, the Thud Factor is Sant's attempt to explain why so many proposal writers feel compelled to produce such lengthy and weighty proposal documents. Lacking any other logical explanation, Sant asserts that some proposal writers believe buyers make purchase decisions based solely on the weight of the proposals submitted; "they drop all of the proposals on a table and the one that makes the biggest 'thud' wins."

While Sant's logic is unassailable, little research has so far been presented to confirm whether proposal weight, thud volume, or measurable seismic disruptions are actually used in strategic purchase decisions.

Unsolicited proposal

An unsolicited proposal is a proposal sent to a buyer that is not in response to a formal procurement document such as an RFI, RFP, or RFQ. Often, a salesperson is speaking with a buyer, and the buyer says something like, "this is interesting, I want to show it to others, please send me a proposal." Even though they ask for it, it's still generally considered unsolicited in the sense it was not requested in response to a formal solicitation.

An unsolicited proposal can also refer to assertive romantic propositions made to pretty girls by ugly guys who, based on a prodigious consumption of alcohol prior, believe they actually have a shot.

Recommended Reading

As a business development person who has one foot in the proposal world and another in the selling world, I've had the benefit of reading some really great books from both realms. Here are my favorites that all BD people involved with formal procurements should read.

Secrets of the Selection Committee. Gary Coover

As the name suggests, Secrets of the Selection Committee is written by someone who has been on many selection committees. In other words, it's not some pie-in-the-sky dissertation about how the process should work, it's a real-life account that explains how it actually does work. He finishes up with his "42 secrets" that all sellers should know about selection committees. These secrets, alone, are worth the price of the book. Buy this book.

Persuasive Business Proposals. Tom Sant

Now in its third edition, Tom's quintessential handbook on proposal writing should be required reading for all proposal development staff, from part-time proposal writers to proposal managers to SMEs who are conscripted into the proposal development process. Buy it, read it, learn from it.

Influence. Robert Cialdini

Everyone who is in the sales or business development profession should read this book, including anyone who writes proposals. If you want to sell stuff, knowing how people make decisions is an important precursor. It's vital. Cialdini tells you how people make decisions. Get the book.

New Sales. Simplified. Mike Weinberg

I preach to my clients that a sale is typically made in the 12 to 24 months before an RFP is released. If you don't know what the decision makers care about, if you only know what's written in an RFP, you don't know much.

New Sales. Simplified. should be required reading for all new business development professionals. Mike teaches you how to reach out to buyers, proactively, so you can start selling at that critical point when buyers are actually making their decisions. And, to be clear, that critical point is long before they issue the RFP.

Proposal Best Practices. David Seibert (me)

Sure, I wrote it. Still, I like the book because it's genuine. It's a 'how to' manual that originated in the real-life trenches of deadline-driven proposal adventures and misadventures. It's filled with lots of practical advice while also including some light-hearted humor along the way. Laugh and learn.

Index

11th hour decision maker, 227
Active voice, 163
AEC industry, 227
APMP. See Association of Proposal
  Management Professionals
Association of Proposal Management
  Professionals, 227
Benefit statements, 166
Bid/No bid decision making, 113
  buyer familiarity, 116
  competitive assessment, 121
  production capacity, 123
  profitability, 125
  proposal team capacity, 124
  requirements, 120
  timing, 114
Business development manager, role
  of, 27
Capture management, 228
Carroll, Lewis, 12
Chunking, 228
Color teams, 228
Column fodder, 229
Competitive proposals, 191
  analyzing, 193
  requesting copies of, 192
Configuring your message, 154
  competitive advantages, 158
  competitors advantages, 159

next five top issues, 155
perceptions of risk, 162
Primary issue, 154
shortcomings, 161
what will it take to win, 166
writing style and tone, 163
Discovery status meeting, *104*
  targeted selling plan, 109
  what are the big tasks remaining?, 106
  what do you know?, 104
  what do you still need to learn?, 105
  what recommendations to make?, 108
Discovery, educating them about you,
  87
  create selling tools, 90
Discovery, learning about them, 75
  document requirements and
    motivations, 79
  document the program, 75
  document their decision model and
    criteria, 84
  how important is price?, 86
  identify reasons for bidding now, 81
  identify the decision makers, 77
FOIA. *See* Freedom of Information
  Act
Formal procurement, 229
Formal procurements, 9
Freedom of Information Act, 191
Ghosting, 230

Ghosting (the competition), 161, 194
Gross win ratio, 230
IDIQ, 230
Informal procurement, 231
Kickoff meetings, 231
National Freedom of Information
    Coalition, 192
No bid, how to, 126
Phase 1
    Prospecting for new opportunities, 12
Phase 2
    Pre-RFP selling, 13
Phase 3
    Proposal development, 14
Phase 4
    Post-proposal selling, 16
Phase 5
    Post-proposal research and analysis, 17
Post procurement review
    buyer interviews, 196
    competitive proposals, 191
Post proposal research and analysis,
    179
    calculating win rates, 183
    debrief your staff, 181
Post proposal selling, 169
Post-RFP buyer interviews, 197
    interview planning, 197
    rules and guidelines, 200
Post-RFP debriefs, 197
Presentation development, 171
Presentation win ratio, 231
Presentations, post proposal
    messaging continuity, 171
    operations staff as presenters, 172
    structure, 174
    tips, 177
Prime contractor, 232
Probability of winning, 232
Procurement types
    formal procurement, 229
    informal procurement, 231
Proposal kickoff meeting, 135, 145
    compiling what you know, 136
    compiling what you've learned, 135

configuring your message, 151
configuring your solution, 145
transforming information into
    intelligence, 139
Proposal planning and development,
    111
Protesting, 232
PWin. See Probability of winning
Qualifying (an opportunity), 233
Qualifying an opportunity, 1
Recompetes, 205
    how to win more, 208
    incumbent advantages, 206
Recurring contracts, 43, 234
    finding, 44
    researching, 48
Request for information, 234
Request for proposal, 234
Request for qualifications, 234
Request for quote, 235
RFI. See Request for information
RFP. See Request for proposal
RFP Selling Process, The, 9
RFQ, 235, See Request for
    qualifications, See Request for
    quote
Sant, Tom
    Thud Factor, 237
Scrutinizing the RFP, 129
    clarity, 133
    favoring a competitor, 131
    requirements and specs, 130
    scoring, 131
    showstoppers, 130
    vs. expectations, 129
    vs. previous RFPs, 132
Selling tool topics, 92
    company background abstracts, 94
    customer case studies, 94
    popular industry topics, 93
    product-specific feature highlights, 92
    product-specific frequently asked
        questions, 93
Selling tools, 90
    blog posts, 92
    documents, 90

podcasts, 91
videos, 91
webinars, 91
Selling tools, guidelines for creating, 95
Short list win ratio, 235
Shortlist, 235
Skimmability, 236
SLED, 236
SME. See Subject matter expert
Solicited proposal, 236
Subcontractor, 236
Subject matter expert, 237
Targeted selling plan, 109
Ten characteristics of formal procurements, 21
Thud factor, 237
Unexpected RFPs
chance of winning, 215

decision discipline, 216
evaluate the situation, 216
options, 218
streamlined kickoff meeting, 224
Unsolicited proposal, 238
Win ratios
gross win ratio, 184
incorporating revenue into calculation, 189
incumbent win ratio, 184
new opportunity win ratio, 184
presentation win ratio, 185
RFP response ratio, 186
segregating ratios by type, 189
short list win ratio, 185
shot in the dark proposal response ratio, 188
shot in the dark proposal win ratio, 188
Writing style and tone, 163

www.ingramcontent.com/pod-product-compliance
Lightning Source LLC
Chambersburg PA
CBHW071347210326
41597CB00015B/1562